D1395022

FAMOUS
IRISH
WRITERS

FAMOUS
IRISH
WRITERS

Martin Wallace

APPLETREE PRESS

First published in 1999
by The Appletree Press Ltd,
The Old Potato Station,
14 Howard Street South,
Belfast BT7 1AP
Tel: +44 (0) 28 90 243074
Fax: +44 (0) 28 90 246756
Web Site: www.irelandseye.com
E-mail: reception@appletree.ie

FAMOUS
IRISH
WRITERS

A catalogue record for this book is available
from the British Library.

ISBN 0-86281-758-7

9 8 7 6 5 4 3 2 1

INTRODUCTION

What do I mean by "famous Irish writers"? By writers I obviously mean Sheridan and Synge and Wilde and other great playwrights. I mean the poet W. B. Yeats, and novelists like Maria Edgeworth and James Joyce. When one thinks of Ireland's remarkable contribution to English literature, such names come immediately to mind. But I have not confined myself to works of fiction or poetic imagination, so there is a place for writers such as Edmund Burke and the historian Lecky and the essayist Robert Lynd.

By Irish, I mean writers born in Ireland or of Irish parentage. Additionally, I have usually looked for some Irish element in their writing, whether in subject matter or style. This has allowed me to exclude someone as famous as Laurence Sterne, author of *Tristram Shandy*, son of an army officer stationed in Ireland but otherwise essentially English. There are, of course, degrees of fame. Some of the writers in this book have remained famous for a century or more – much more in the case of a Swift or a Goldsmith. Some have enjoyed briefer periods of celebrity, though often retaining a smaller but devoted following- Charles Lever, perhaps, or George A. Birmingham. You will not often see Charles Kickham's name in works on English literature, but his novel *Knocknagow* has deservedly been famous among generations of Irish readers.

I have included only authors who have achieved fame by writing in the English language. There is no Brian Merriman, for example, for he wrote in Irish, and his wider fame rests on other writers' translations of *The Midnight Court*. But you will find Brendan Behan and Walter Macken, who used both Irish and English – not to mention Samuel Beckett, who latterly wrote in French before translating his work. There is no place for Saint Patrick, of course, for his *Confession* is in Latin.

Dates in parenthesis almost always indicate the year in which a play was first staged or a book first published. Some plays were written and even (notably in Bernard Shaw's case) published years before their first production; many novels were first serialised in magazines. I have in some instances drawn attention to small museums specialising in a particular writer's life and work. These are worth visiting, as is the Writers' Museum in Parnell Square, Dublin.

JONATHAN SWIFT

1667–1745

Swift, whose parents were English, was born in Dublin on 30 November 1667. His mother had been widowed some months earlier, and she returned to her family in Leicestershire. A wealthy uncle secured Swift's education at Kilkenny College and Trinity College, Dublin, where he graduated in 1686. Three years later he became private secretary to Sir William Temple of Moor Park in Surrey.

Swift spent much of the following decade at Moor Park, and after Temple's death in 1699 he edited his patron's papers. He also spent some time in Ireland, taking holy orders in 1694. He was appointed to the parish of Kilroot, Co. Antrim, but returned to Surrey in 1696. His duties at Moor Park now included tutoring Hester Johnson, the "Stella" of his writing and possibly Temple's child. One theory suggests that Swift's real father was Sir John Temple, Sir William's father and a former master of the Irish rolls, so that Swift and Stella might have been blood relatives.

Swift returned to Ireland as domestic chaplain to the Earl of Berkeley, lately appointed a lord justice, and in 1700 he also became vicar of Laracor, near Trim, Co. Meath. After Berkeley was recalled in 1701, Swift became a frequent visitor to England, acquiring a reputation as a wit and pamphleteer. Stella, who had benefited from Temple's will, was persuaded to move to Ireland and thereafter lived close to Swift's residences in Laracor or Dublin.

In 1704 Swift published *A Tale of a Tub*, which he described as a satire on "the numerous and gross corruptions in religion and learning", and which defended the Church of England as a middle ground of Christianity. Simultaneously, *The Battle of the Books*, originally written to support Temple's views, defended classical literature. In 1707 Swift was commissioned by the Church of Ireland to negotiate a relief of taxes levied on the clergy. Although he had good connections among the governing Whigs, he was initially unsuccessful. When the Tories introduced relief in 1710, Swift changed his political allegiance. He edited the Tory journal *The Examiner* during 1710–11 and enjoyed political influence until the death of Queen Anne in 1714, though without receiving any ecclesiastical preferment.

Swift's *Journal to Stella* was written during 1710–13 and provides a lively account of London life. He became a frequent visitor to the home of Esther Vanhomrigh, whose widowed mother had moved from Dublin to London. The young woman became infatuated with Swift and followed him to Ireland.

She became the "Vanessa" of his long poem *Cadmus and Vanessa*, written in 1713 but only published in 1726, three years after her death.

In 1713 Swift became dean of St Patrick's Cathedral in Dublin. He had hoped for a bishopric and felt himself exiled, particularly when the Whigs returned to power. Eventually he turned his savage pen to Irish problems. In 1720 he published *A Proposal for the Universal Use of Irish Manufacture*, advising: "Burn everything that comes from England except the coal". In his anonymous series of *Drapier's Letters* (1724) he successfully resisted the introduction of a corrupt new currency known as "Wood's halfpence". *A Modest Proposal* (1729), directed at Ireland's governing class during a time of famine, suggested bitterly that the country's starving babies might be sold to feed the rich, their skins providing "admirable gloves for the ladies, and summer boots for fine gentlemen".

Meanwhile Swift had published his famous *Gulliver's Travels* (1726). Much of the book was recognisably a satire on contemporary society, but its moral lessons have proved durable. Moreover, Lemuel Gulliver's adventures among Lilliputians, Brobdingnagians, Laputans, Houyhnhnms, Yahoos and other strange creatures have ensured the book's survival as a classic of children's literature. *Gulliver's Travels* ultimately takes a gloomy view of mankind, and Swift's later years were certainly unhappy ones. Stella, the "truest, most virtuous and most valuable friend", died in 1727. Swift, suffering from Ménière's disease, described himself as "Deaf, giddy, helpless, left alone". He was committed to the care of guardians in 1742 and died in Dublin on 19 October 1745.

SIR RICHARD STEELE

1672–1729

Steele, son of an attorney, was born in Dublin in 1672. He was educated at Charterhouse, where he met his lifelong friend Joseph Addison, and at Oxford, but left to enter the army. In 1701 he published *Christian Hero*, a pious treatise which found public favour but displeased his fellow officers. "From being thought no undelightful Companion," Steele later wrote, "he was soon reckoned a disagreeable Fellow".

It was to "enliven his Character" that he wrote a comedy, *The Funeral* (1701), which was staged at Drury Lane, as were *The Lying Lover* (1703) and *The Tender Husband* (1705). The plays adopted a moral tone which contrasted with the works of his contemporaries, but only the first had much success, and Steele was to say that *The Lying Lover* was "damn'd for its Piety".

On 12 April 1709 the first issue of the *Tatler* appeared, drawing material from London's coffee houses: "Accounts of Gallantry, Pleasure and Entertainment" from White's, poetry from Will's, learning from the Grecian, and news from the St James's. Steele had found his métier as an essayist, and Addison soon became a contributor, but the last issue was published in January 1711.

On 1 March 1711 the daily *Spectator* appeared. Addison first delineated the "looker-on" of the title, and Steele then introduced the members of the imaginary Club for which he and the journal are best known: the merchant Sir Andrew Freeport, Captain Sentry, gallant Will Honeycomb, and especially Sir Roger de Coverley, the Worcestershire gentleman crossed in love by a perverse widow. The *Spectator* was published until December 1712, reaching a daily circulation of 10,000, and Steele was to launch several other short-lived journals.

During his life Steele held several public appointments, only to lose them on falling out of political favour. He became MP for Stockbridge, Hampshire, in 1713, but his pamphlet on the Hanoverian succession led to his expulsion from Westminster in 1714. When George I succeeded Queen Anne, his fortunes rose. In 1715 he received £1,000 a year to run Drury Lane, returned to parliament and was knighted. In 1718 he received a patent for a "fish pool" to bring live salmon from Ireland, but the venture failed. Steele's comedy *The Conscious Lovers* was a success in 1722, but financial difficulties forced him out of London, and he died at Carmarthen on 1 September 1729.

GEORGE FARQUHAR

| 1677–1707

Farquhar, a clergyman's son, was born in Derry in 1677. He entered Trinity College, Dublin, in 1694 but left within two years, probably for financial reasons. Soon afterwards he was taken on as an actor in the nearby Smock Alley theatre, showing some talent for comedy. In 1697 he was cast in Dryden's *Indian Emperor* and accidentally ran his sword into a fellow actor. The wounded man recovered, but Farquhar determined not to act again.

The Dublin actor Robert Wilks advised him to try writing comedies, and Farquhar set off for London, where the bawdy plays of Wycherley, Congreve and Vanbrugh were in vogue. His first play, *Love and a Bottle*, was well received at Drury Lane in 1698. *The Constant Couple, or A Trip to the Jubilee* (1699) was partly inspired by festivities marking the jubilee of Pope Innocent XII and enjoyed a long run. Wilks took the leading role, an "airy gentleman affecting humorous gaiety and freedom" who provided the title of Farquhar's next play, *Sir Harry Wildair* (1701).

Farquhar's finances were usually precarious, and he had little success with *The Inconstant* (1702), *The Twin Rivals* (1702) and *The Stage-Coach* (1703). He had married a widow with two children in 1703, only to find she was not an heiress as he had thought. Consequently, in 1704 he took up a lieutenant's commission in a foot regiment raised by his friend George Boyle, an unsuccessful playwright who had succeeded to the earldom of Orrery. He was sent on a recruiting mission to Shropshire, an experience from which he wrote *The Recruiting Officer* (1706), with the approval of Orrery and his general, the Duke of Ormonde.

Farquhar remained in debt despite the play's success, and his health was failing. Ormonde advised him to sell his commission. Wilks, his constant friend, lent him twenty guineas and he drew again on his Shropshire experiences to write *The Beaux' Stratagem* (1707), which opened to acclaim at the Haymarket theatre. These last two plays were his best, with a rural realism and high spirits supplanting the more artificial comedy of the earlier plays. They were also the last of the great Restoration comedies, for Wycherley, Congreve and Vanbrugh had already turned to other ventures. Farquhar's decline continued and he died on 29 April 1707.

GEORGE BERKELEY

1685–1753

Berkeley was born in Co. Kilkenny on 12 March 1685. He was educated at Kilkenny College and at Trinity College, Dublin, where he graduated in 1704. In 1707 Berkeley was elected a fellow of TCD, and in 1710 he took holy orders.

Berkeley's major contributions to philosophy, which brought him a reputation throughout Europe, were written over a short period of time. His first work, *An Essay towards a New Theory of Vision* (1709), was concerned with the manner in which objects are perceived by sight. His masterpiece, *A Treatise concerning the Principles of Human Knowledge*, appeared in 1710 and its arguments were expounded in a more popular form in *Three Dialogues between Hylas and Philonous* (1713).

Berkeley's philosophy emerged primarily as a criticism of the work of John Locke and Isaac Newton, though in most respects he admired their achievements. Locke's famous *Essay on Human Understanding* had quickly entered the TCD philosophy course, and Berkeley sought to reveal errors in its reasoning. In particular, he denied the existence of matter and, describing himself as an "immaterialist", argued that things depended for their existence on being perceived: *esse est percipi*

In 1713 Berkeley took leave of absence and went to London, where he was quickly taken up by Swift, Steele (*see pages 6 & 8*), Addison, Pope and other wits of the coffee houses. He also travelled extensively in Europe before returning to Dublin in 1721. In 1724 he became dean of Derry and soon embarked on a project to establish a college in Bermuda for the education of young Indians and to prepare colonists' sons for the ministry.

In 1728 Berkeley sailed to Newport, Rhode Island, where he bought a farm, but returned to England in 1731 when he was advised that a promised government grant for the college would never materialise. Berkeley was by then as popular among American intellectuals as he had been in England, and on leaving he made gifts to Yale and Harvard universities.

In 1734 Berkeley was appointed bishop of Cloyne, Co. Cork. His mind turned increasingly to Irish problems, and in the three volumes of *The Querist* (1735–7) he posed almost six-hundred cogent questions about social and economic conditions in the country. Ill health forced his retirement in 1752, and he moved to Oxford where he died on 14 January 1753.

OLIVER GOLDSMITH

1728–1774

Accounts of Goldsmith's birth vary, but a family Bible suggests it was at Pallas, Co. Longford, on 18 November 1728. His father became rector of nearby Kilkenny West in 1730, and Goldsmith was reared at Lissoy parsonage in Co. Westmeath. He was much influenced by the local schoolmaster, Thomas Byrne, a widely travelled ex-soldier whom he recalled in his poem *The Deserted Village.* "And still they gazed, and still the wonder grew, That one small head could carry all he knew".

In 1745 Goldsmith entered Trinity College, Dublin, as a sizar or poor scholar. His academic career was undistinguished, and on graduating in 1749 he pursued an idle life at home. He thought of taking holy orders like his father and elder brother, but his application was rejected. In 1752 Goldsmith set off for Edinburgh to study medicine, but left in 1754 and continued his studies at Leyden in Holland. In 1755, still unqualified, he embarked on a walking tour through France, Switzerland, Italy and probably Germany. A year later he arrived penniless in London, where he found work as an apothecary's assistant, physician and schoolmaster before drifting into journalism.

In 1759 Goldsmith published *An Enquiry into the Present State of Polite Learning,* an examination of the literary scene in England and some European countries. With a growing reputation, he published biographies of Voltaire (1761) and Beau Nash (1762). His first popular success was *Letters of a Citizen of the World* (1762), a compilation of his "Chinese Letters" in the *Public Register,* which purported to be the reflections of a Chinese philosopher visiting London. Within a year he became a founder member of Samuel Johnson's famous Club, which met in the Turk's Head in Soho.

Goldsmith's poem *The Traveller* (1764) was considered by Johnson the best English poem since the death of Alexander Pope. It was dedicated to his brother Henry, the modest cleric who had "left the field of ambition, where the labours are many, and the harvest not worth carrying away". The long poem, inspired by Goldsmith's earlier travels, is a philosophical search for the "particular principle of happiness" of each country he views. He could see that English life was changing as industry and commerce expanded, and rightly foresaw that revolutionary forces might be unleashed. *The Vicar of Wakefield* followed in 1766. According to James Boswell's account, Goldsmith had been arrested for not paying his rent, but was released after Johnson sold the manuscript for £60. The novel is narrated by Dr Primrose, an unworldly cleric whose family suffers many reverses – notably at the hands of Squire Thornhill, who seduces his elder daughter – before attaining a happy prosperity. A masterpiece of romantic comedy, it has since been translated into many languages.

Goldsmith's first play, *The Good-natur'd Man* (1768), enjoyed modest success at Covent Garden. It is not hard to see a reflection of Goldsmith himself in the hero of this sentimental comedy, a young man whose generosity and extravagance forever threaten him with a debtors' prison.

In 1770 Goldsmith's poem *The Deserted Village* went quickly into five editions. It deals with rural depopulation, contrasting the needy poor with opulent and indolent landlords: "Ill fares the land, to hastening ills a prey, Where wealth accumulates, and men decay". Goldsmith's "Sweet Auburn! Loveliest village of the plain" was drawn from his memories of Lissoy.

Goldsmith's reputation as a playwright was secured by *She Stoops to Conquer* (1773). As a young man, Goldsmith had sought lodgings in a country house, mistaking it for an inn; in his farce, the young suitor Marlow unknowingly treats his prospective father-in-law Hardcastle as a landlord and his bride as a servant. Hardcastle's stepson, the idle and mischievous Tony Lumpkin, is a memorable creation.

Beset by debt, Goldsmith died in London on 4 April 1774 and was buried in Westminster Abbey. Johnson wrote his epitaph: *"Nullum quod tetigit non ornavit"* (He touched nothing which he did not adorn). David Garrick's version was "Here lies Nolly Goldsmith, for shortness call'd Noll, Who wrote like an angel, but talk'd like poor Poll".

EDMUND BURKE

1729–1797

Burke was born in Dublin, probably on 1 January 1729. On graduating from Trinity College, Dublin, in 1748 he studied law at the Middle Temple in London. Seeking a literary career, he published A *Vindication* of *Natural Society* (1756), a satire on rationalist philosophy, and *Origin of our Ideas of the Sublime and Beautiful* (1757), a treatise on aesthetics. Burke was quickly taken up by Goldsmith, Sheridan (*see pages 11 & 14*), Reynolds and other worthies, and was a founder member of Samuel Johnson's Club. In 1758 he was invited to edit the first *Annual Register* and continued to do so for almost twenty years.

In 1761 Burke became private secretary to the chief secretary in Ireland, W. G. Hamilton. After a breach with Hamilton in 1765, he became private secretary to Lord Rockingham, who briefly headed a Whig administration at Westminster. He entered parliament in 1766 as MP for Wendover and later sat for Bristol – losing that seat for insisting that he was a representative of his constituents and not their delegate – and Malton.

Burke had a distinguished parliamentary career, raising the standard of debate and fostering the party system. He took the lead in impeaching Warren Hastings, the former governor-general of India, in 1787. Though he never held a major office of state, his views have influenced politicians for two centuries.

Burke was also an active pamphleteer. *Thoughts on the Cause of the Present Discontents* (1770) challenged George III's misuse of his powers; Burke then contributed to the debate on America in *Conciliation with the Colonies* (1775) and *Letter to the Sheriffs of Bristol* (1777). Having vainly urged a conciliatory approach in America, Burke argued that the government should not repeat its mistakes in Ireland. *A Letter to a Peer of Ireland* (1782) criticised the penal laws against Roman Catholics, and his *Letter to Sir Hercules Langrishe* (1792) called for Catholic emancipation.

Burke's best-known work is *Reflections on the Revolution in France* (1790), in which he foresaw the dangers which events in France posed to the ordered liberty of England. His views led to a breach with Whig friends, such as Sheridan and Charles James Fox, and to Thomas Paine's famous reply, *Rights of Man* (1792). Burke retired from parliament in 1794 and died at Beaconsfield, in Buckinghamshire, on 9 July 1797.

RICHARD BRINSLEY SHERIDAN

Sheridan was born in Dublin on 30 October 1751. His father was Thomas Sheridan, actor-manager of the Theatre Royal in Smock Alley and later lexicographer and biographer of Jonathan Swift (*see page 6*). His mother Frances Sheridan (*née* Chamberlaine), was an actress who became a successful novelist, notably with *The Memoirs of Miss Sidney Biddulph* (1761), and playwright. The uncertainties of Dublin theatre persuaded Thomas Sheridan to pursue his other great interest, the promotion of an education system which emphasised elocution and oratory, and he subsequently moved to England. His son continued his schooling in Dublin for a time, but in 1759 joined his parents in England and never returned to Ireland.

Richard Sheridan spent some unhappy years at Harrow school before moving with his family to Bath in 1770. Two years later, he eloped to France with a fashionable young singer, Eliza Linley, whose engagement to a much older man had recently ended in a breach-of-promise action. The couple went through a form of marriage near Calais but, as both were minors, it proved invalid. They were eventually married in 1773 despite their parents' disapproval. Sheridan's bride had been originally motivated by a desire to escape from another suitor, with whom her husband later duelled twice, incurring severe wounds on the second occasion.

Eliza Sheridan's voice could have given the couple a handsome income, but Sheridan insisted she give up her professional career. He had already contributed some entertaining verses to journals in Bath, and now determined to make a living in the theatre. When his comedy *The Rivals* was staged at Covent Garden in 1775, it was ill received. However, judicious rewriting and a cast change soon ensured the play's success, and characters such as Sir Lucius O'Trigger, Sir Anthony Absolute and Mrs Malaprop have entertained audiences ever since. The play is set in Bath, and Sheridan drew to some extent on his own experiences of youthful romance, parental tyranny and duelling.

Before the year was out, two more works by Sheridan were staged at Covent Garden. *St Patrick's Day*, a farce, starred the Irish actor Laurence Clinch, who had taken over the O'Trigger role. *The Duenna*, a comic opera with music by Thomas Linley, Sheridan's father-in-law, had an unprecedented run of seventy-five performances. In 1776, still only twenty-four, Sheridan succeeded David Garrick as manager of the Theatre Royal in Drury Lane, where all his later plays were staged. A new production of *The Rivals* was followed by *A Trip to Scarborough* (1777), adapted from Sir John Vanbrugh's *The Relapse*. However, it was *The School for Scandal* which later in the year gave Sheridan his greatest triumph. Again, the author provided memorable comic characters, not least the scandal-mongering Lady Sneerwell, Mrs Candour and Sir Benjamin Backbite. The play touched on political issues of the day, and Sheridan had to use his personal influence to persuade the lord chamberlain to grant it a licence.

Sheridan went on to write *The Camp* (1778), a musical entertainment, and *The Critic* (1779), the latter satire featuring such hacks as Dangle, Sneer, Puff and Sir Fretful Plagiary. However, he began to show more interest in politics and in 1780 was elected MP for Stafford, the first of several seats. He held minor offices in Whig administrations, and was a notable parliamentary orator, most famously in a 340-minute speech urging the impeachment of Warren Hastings. Sheridan was sympathetic to both the American and the French revolutions and strongly opposed the union of Great Britain and Ireland.

His only other play was *Pizarro* (1799), adapted from a German tragedy, but he contributed to other productions. In 1809 Drury Lane was destroyed by fire, adding to Sheridan's already substantial financial difficulties, and in 1812 he lost his Westminster seat. Sheridan's wife had died in 1792, and a second marriage in 1795 gave him a less congenial partner. In his last years, beset with debt, Sheridan drank too freely and quarrelled with old friends. He died in London on 7 July 1816 and was buried in Poets' Corner at Westminster Abbey.

SIR JONAH BARRINGTON

| 1760–1834

Barrington was born at Knapton, near Abbeyleix, Queen's County, in 1760. One of sixteen children, he grew up in an Anglo-Irish household not unlike that described by Maria Edgeworth (*see page 17*) in *Castle Rackrent*. Educated at Trinity College, Dublin, he declined an army career and was admitted to the Irish Bar in 1788. Elected to the Irish parliament in 1790, he was an MP for most of the decade preceding the 1800 Act of Union. Barrington voted against the union with Great Britain, by his own account turning down the proffered post of solicitor general, yet apparently had a part in persuading some corrupt politicians to support it.

Barrington's legal career, initially very successful, was not unblemished. He took silk in 1793, became a judge of the admiralty court in 1798, and was knighted in 1807. However, a court of inquiry in 1830 found that he had appropriated money paid into the court, and he was deprived of his office. He had by then left Ireland to escape his creditors and spent his last years in France, dying at Versailles on 8 April 1834.

Fortunately, Barrington's financial difficulties drove him to writing his memoirs to earn money, for no one has given a better account of life among the gentry of eighteenth-century Ireland. Barrington's *Personal Sketches of His Own Times* was published in three volumes (1827–32), and his anecdotes and descriptions are both entertaining and informative. He is a shrewd social commentator, as when he notes the division of gentry into "Half mounted gentlemen; gentlemen every inch of them; and gentlemen to the backbone". Contemporaries such as John Philpot Curran, Henry Grattan and Sir Boyle Roche – the greatest exponent of the Irish "bull", or garbled saying – are as finely and frankly portrayed as in any other account of the period.

Barrington's world is a mixture of elegance and brutality, and violence is never far below the surface. The rituals of duelling occupy some space; not surprisingly, for he fought his first duel at sixteen and later clashed with Leonard McNally, informer and author of "The Lass of Richmond Hill." Barrington also wrote *Historic Memoirs of Ireland* (1833) and *The Rise and Fall of the Irish Nation* (1833). They lack the flair of his principal work, but provide a valuable account of events surrounding the Act of Union.

MARIA EDGEWORTH

1767–1849

Maria Edgeworth was born in Black Bourton in Oxfordshire. The date has been traditionally given as 1 January 1767, but may have been one year later. She was the third child of Richard Lovell Edgeworth by the first of his four wives, and was to be closely associated with her father in his educational work and in bringing up many of his twenty-two children. Most of her childhood was spent in England, but in 1782 she accompanied her father, his third wife and a number of children to Edgeworthstown, Co. Longford.

Her father immediately set himself to improve the neglected Edgeworth estate and proved to be a progressive and humane landlord. He was also an inventor, devising a telegraph, a velocipede, a perambulator for measuring land, a turnip-cutter and a railway to carry limestone. He took an active interest in his children's education, and Maria's first publication, *Letters for Literary Ladies* (1795), owed much to his ideas on women's education. It was followed by *The Parent's Assistant* (1796), a collection of children's stories, and their jointly written *Practical Education* (1798). More children's stories were published in 1801 as *Early Lessons* and *Moral Tales*.

Maria's first and best novel, *Castle Rackrent* (1800), was published anonymously. It achieved immediate success, and her name appeared on subsequent editions. The short novel describes the decline of a family of profligate landlords. Sir Patrick Rackrent drinks himself to death, the litigious Sir Murtagh bursts a blood vessel quarrelling with his wife, the absentee Sir Kit is killed in a duel, and Sir Condy dies after signing away his last claim to the estate. The story is told in dialect by the Rackrents' steward, "honest Thady" Quirk, whose scheming son Jason becomes agent and finally owner of the estate. *Castle Rackrent* has been described as the first regional novel in English. It influenced French and Russian novelists, while Sir Walter Scott hoped in *Waverley* (1814) to "emulate the admirable Irish portraits".

Belinda (1801), a novel of manners describing a young woman's emergence into society, was admired by Jane Austen. It is notable for the portrait of Belinda's sponsor, Lady Delacour, apparently dying of cancer and as witty as she is dissipated. *The Modern Griselda* (1805) and *Leonora* (1806) are studies of marriage, the latter told through letters. By now a celebrated author, Maria Edgeworth then published a series of *Tales of Fashionable Life*, notably *Ennui* (1809) and *The Absentee* (1812), both of which treat the problems of landlordism in Ireland. In *The Absentee* the

17

Clonbrony family are first seen in extravagant London society; their son travels incognito to Ireland and discovers that they are being cheated by a corrupt agent; the family return to Ireland to manage their estates.

Maria Edgeworth had collaborated with her father on *Essay on Irish Bulls* (1802), a collection of sometimes inadvertent humour. The two authors then visited Paris, where she turned down a marriage proposal from a Swedish diplomat. Her father also contributed to the writing of *Ormond* (1817), though he was near death. The novel, inferior only to *Castle Rackrent* among Maria Edgeworth's prolific output, describes the maturing of a wild but clever young Irishman exposed to English and French society. Most notable is the contrast drawn between the cousins O'Shane: the Catholic Cornelius or King Corny living as a feudal Gaelic ruler on a remote island, and the scheming Ulick who has turned Protestant and joined the Anglo-lrish gentry. Two other long novels of this period, *Patronage* (1814) and *Harrington* (1817), were less successful.

Poor eyesight made Maria Edgeworth curtail her reading and writing for a period, and in 1826 she had to take over the management of the Edgeworthstown estate from her ineffectual brother Lovell. Ever the educator and moralist, she wrote several more improving stories for children, but the novel *Helen* (1834) was the only substantial achievement of her later years. Another novel of manners, it features a virtuous orphan whose happiness is threatened by a deceitful friend. Maria Edgeworth died at Edgeworthstown on 22 May 1849.

LADY MORGAN

1776?–1859

By her own account, Sydney Owenson was born in Dublin on 25 December 1785, but a likelier year is 1776, and the birth may have taken place on the Irish Sea. Her father was the Irish actor Robert Owenson, lately returned from Drury Lane in London. She was briefly a governess before prospering as a novelist.

Owenson published *St Clair* (1802), *The Novice of St Dominick* (1805) and a collection of *Twelve Original Hibernian Melodies* (1805) before establishing a lasting reputation with *The Wild Irish Girl* (1806). In the novel a young Englishman discovers that an ancient Gaelic civilisation survives in the West of Ireland; his mentor is Glorvina, daughter of a dispossessed Milesian prince. The book successfully exploited the nationalist feelings which had survived the failure of the 1798 rising, and was a success on both sides of the Irish Sea.

A comic opera, *The First Attempt* (1807), was followed by the more serious *Patriotic Sketches* (1807), which considered the causes of Catholic poverty. *Woman, or Ida of Athens* (1809) had echoes of Ireland in portraying Greek rebellion against Turkey. Owenson accepted an invitation to join the household of the Marquis of Abercorn, and it was at his Baron's Court estate in Co. Tyrone that she met her future husband, Charles Morgan, an English doctor. Abercorn persuaded the lord lieutenant to knight Morgan, and after some reluctance Owenson married in 1812. The couple extricated themselves from the Abercorn household and settled in Dublin.

In *O'Donnel* (1814), involving a soldier of fortune and a governess, Lady Morgan fictionalises the Abercorns and other contemporaries. The novel's success produced a commission to write *France* (1817); with Napoleon gone, English travellers were again visiting the Continent, and Lady Morgan was feted in Paris. A similar work on *Italy* (1821) followed. Meanwhile *Florence Macarthy* (1819) raised questions of national identity in Ireland, ending with an alliance between a Gaelic countess and a descendant of Norman aristocracy.

Her best novel, *The O'Briens and the O'Flahertys* (1827), is a panoramic view of the period leading to the 1798 rising. A romantic nationalist, Lady Morgan was unhappy with Daniel O'Connell's sectarian methods of pursuing Catholic emancipation, and she found Dublin increasingly prudish. In 1837, the government granted her a literary pension of £300, and she settled in London where she died on 16 April 1859.

THOMAS MOORE

1779–1852

Moore, the son of a prosperous Roman Catholic grocer, was born in Dublin on 28 May 1779. In 1795 he entered Trinity College, Dublin, where his friends included Robert Emmet and Edward Hudson, both members of the illegal United Irishmen movement. Moore himself avoided the conspiracy; in 1797 he was questioned by college authorities seeking to purge Trinity of rebels, but would only answer questions about himself. He was allowed to remain and graduated in 1798.

While at school, Moore had published verses in *Anthologia Hibernica*, and at TCD he embarked on translating works attributed to the Greek poet Anacreon. It was Hudson, later exiled after the 1798 rising failed, who awakened Moore's interest in Irish music, particularly in the collection of Irish harpists' airs published by Edward Bunting in 1796. Emmet, executed in 1803, inspired two of Moore's most memorable ballads, "O breathe not his name" and "She is far from the land where her young lover sleeps".

In 1799, planning a legal career, Moore entered the Middle Temple in London. A fortunate meeting with the Earl of Moira provided him with a patron who introduced him to London society, where Moore's singing was soon in great demand. When *Odes of Anacreon* was published in 1800, Moore was permitted to dedicate the volume to the Prince Regent.

In 1803 Moira proposed that his protégé become the first poet laureate of Ireland, but Moore was modest enough to decline the offer. However, he did accept another sinecure arranged by Moira and sailed to Bermuda as admiralty registrar. Appointing a deputy, he soon returned to London, where in 1808 he published his first volume of *Irish Melodies*, with music arranged by Sir John Stevenson. Another nine volumes were to follow, the last in 1834; Moore's publishing contract required him regularly to perform the songs.

The *Melodies* were an immediate success and remain the work by which he is best known. They include songs such as "Believe me if all those endearing young charms", "The last rose of summer", "The harp that once through Tara's halls", "The meeting of the waters" and "The minstrel boy". He was equally popular in Ireland, giving musical expression to the growing sense of Irish nationhood. Moore also published, with less success, six volumes of *National Airs* (1818–27), including "Oft in the stilly night", and "two of Sacred Songs" (1816–24), and composed a comic opera *M.P., or the Blue Stocking* (1811).

Moore's poetry is little read today, though it was popular in its time. *Lalla Rookh* (1817) went into its seventh edition within a year, but modern critics find this oriental narrative poem inferior to the work of contemporaries such as Wordsworth or Shelley. *The Loves of the Angels* (1823) dealt with three fallen angels expelled from heaven; in later editions, responding to criticism, Moore turned them into seraphs expelled from their Moslem paradise. He also wrote satirical and polemic verse, notably in *Intercepted Letters, or the Two-Penny Post Bag* (1813), supposedly the letters of Tory politicians, and *The Fudge Family in Paris* (1818).

In 1811 Moore married a young actress, Bessie Dyke; the marriage was a happy one, marred only by the early deaths of their five children and by frequent financial difficulties. In 1819 Moore fled to France for three years to escape a debtor's prison, after his deputy in Bermuda had stolen £6,000. While abroad, he was entrusted with the memoirs of his close friend Lord Byron, but sold the copyright and so allowed Byron's family to have them destroyed after the poet's death. Moore published a biography of Byron in 1830 and also wrote lives of Richard Brinsley Sheridan (1825) (*see page 14*) and the Irish rebel, Lord Edward Fitzgerald (1831). His historical novel *Memoirs of Captain Rock* (1824) exposed Irish grievances and forwarded the cause of Catholic emancipation.

Moore's popularity in Ireland was such that he was approached to stand for parliament, but he disliked Daniel O'Connell's demagoguery and declined the offers. In later life he lived in Sloperton, Wiltshire, where he died on 25 February 1852.

CHARLES ROBERT MATURIN

1780–1824

Maturin was born in Dublin on 25 September 1780. His middle-class family were of Huguenot stock, and his forbears included a dean of Killala and the successor to Jonathan Swift (*see page 6*) as dean of St Patrick's. He graduated from Trinity College, Dublin, in 1800, was ordained as a minister in 1803 and in 1804 became curate of Loughrea, Co. Galway. Within a year, he had become curate of St Peter's in Dublin, where he remained until his death on 30 October 1824.

His first novel, *The Fatal Revenge, or the Family of Montorio*, was published in 1807 at his own expense. It is an Italian tale of murder, madness and deception in the Gothic tradition popularised in the late eighteenth century by Mrs Anne Radcliffe and Monk Lewis. The novel was ill-received – "too defective in female characters and female interest" wrote Maturin – and its successor, *The Wild Irish Boy* (1808), was patently an attempt to emulate the success of Lady Morgan (*see page 19*). His least effective work, it has some merit in depicting Ormsby Bethel's passion for the older Lady Montrevor.

The author's finances declined when his father was dismissed from the Irish Post Office. He also lost money through a relative's insolvency. His unorthodox novels must have denied him clerical promotion, and he was glad to earn £80 for *The Milesian Chief* (1812), a tragic romance set in the unsettled period following the 1798 rising. A correspondence with Sir Walter Scott encouraged Maturin to submit a melodrama, *Bertram*, to the Drury Lane Theatre in London, and in 1816 it enjoyed great success with Edmund Kean as an aristocratic bandit. His later plays, *Manuel* (1817) and *Fredolfo* (1819), were failures.

Fortunately, the novel *Women, or Pour et Contre* (1818) proved a masterly combination of the Gothic and the romantic, depicting the psychological and physical aspects of love, while criticising the Calvinism which, by inhibiting the young heroine Eva Wentworth, drives young Charles De Courcy towards the mature actress Zaira Dalmatiani. Even more successful was *Melmoth the Wanderer* (1820), on which Maturin's reputation largely rests. A powerful series of tales drawing on the legends of the Wandering Jew and of Faust, it influenced such writers as Balzac and Baudelaire. A final historical novel, *The Albigenses* (1824), clearly owes a debt to Scott's *Ivanhoe*.

22

WILLIAM CARLETON

1794–1869

Carleton was born at Prillisk, near Clogher, Co. Tyrone, on 20 February 1794. His Roman Catholic father was a small farmer, fluent in both English and Irish, whom Carleton found a storehouse of folklore and antiquarian knowledge. The last of fourteen children, Carleton attended hedge-schools, and on his father's death it was decided that he should be educated for the priesthood.

In 1812 he set out for Munster, but got no farther than Granard, Co. Longford, where he had a frightening dream that a mad bull was pursuing him. The superstitious Carleton took this as a bad omen and returned home; in 1817 a pilgrimage to Lough Derg, Co. Donegal, finally decided him against taking holy orders. During 1814–16 Carleton attended a classical school in Glaslough, Co. Monaghan. Returning to his family, he lived an idle life, indulging his taste for dancing and athletic sports. Eventually, inspired by reading the picaresque novel *Gil Blas*, Carleton set off to seek his fortune.

Living precariously, Carleton tutored in Co. Louth, ran a hedge-school in Newcastle, Co. Dublin, and finally arrived in Dublin. With little money in his pocket, he lived among the city's beggars before finding work as a tutor with an evangelical Protestant, whose niece he married in 1822. He taught in Mullingar, Co. Westmeath, and in Carlow before returning to Dublin.

By now Carleton was an opponent of Catholic emancipation and of the Roman Catholic Church and he was invited to contribute to the *Christian Examiner*, edited by Rev. Caesar Otway. He began with an account of his Lough Derg pilgrimage and drew on his experiences in other sketches of rural life, often portraying the superstition of Irish Catholics and the power of their clergy. A collection of *Traits and Stories of the Irish Peasantry* was published in 1830, followed by a second series in 1833 and *Tales of Ireland* in 1834, by which time Carleton had severed his connection with the fiery Otway.

During the 1830s the *Dublin University Magazine* serialised several novels, but nothing appeared under the brief editorship of Charles Lever (*see page 30*), whom Carleton accused of plagiarism and offering "disgusting and debasing caricatures of Irish life". The Banim brothers (*see page 27*) were among his admirers; Carleton applied unsuccessfully for John Banim's civil pension after the latter died, but did eventually receive a pension in 1848.

His first novel, *Fardorougha the Miser*, appeared in book form in 1839, and Carleton soon became a popular author. His later novels include

Valentine M'Clutchy (1845), on eviction, and showing a new sympathy towards the Catholic clergy and the nationalist cause; *Rody the Rover* (1845), on Ribbonmen, the secret Catholic society into which Carleton had been initiated as a young man; *The Black Prophet* (1847), on an earlier potato famine than the one then being experienced; and *The Emigrants of Aghadarra* (1847).

Even with a pension, Carleton's finances were usually in disarray, and he never enjoyed good terms from his Irish publishers. His later novels are generally inferior to those dealing topically with Ireland's profound problems, but he had a popular success with his sentimental *Willy Reilly and his Dear Colleen Bawn* (1855). Carleton's autobiography was incomplete when he died in Dublin on 30 January 1869, but his account of his early years was finally published in 1896. Carleton was out of fashion for some years until W. B. Yeats (*see page 52*) described him as "the greatest novelist of Ireland by right of the most Celtic eyes that ever gazed from under the brows of a story-teller". If this was too generous an evaluation, Carleton nonetheless demands respect for the manner in which he recorded the language of a people who, while giving up the Irish language, preserved its rhythms and grammatical structures in their use of English. Moreover, in his descriptions of poor scholar, matchmaker, country fiddler, dancing master and others, and in the violence of stories such as "The Battle of the Factions" and "Wildgoose Hall", he has left an unequalled gallery of rural portraits.

MICHAEL AND JOHN BANIM

1796–1874 1798–1842

Both brothers were born in Kilkenny, Michael on 5 August1796 and John on
3 April 1798. Their father was a Catholic farmer with a business selling
fowling pieces and fishing rods. The older son had to give up legal ambitions
to help his father; the younger, on leaving Kilkenny College, studied in Dublin
before becoming a drawing teacher in Kilkenny. An abortive romance soon
cast a shadow over his life. The young girl was removed from Kilkenny by an
irate father and died of consumption, whereupon the despairing Banim
contracted the spinal tuberculosis which eventually killed him.

In 1820, John Banim returned to Dublin, abandoning art for literature.
In 1821 he published a long poem, *The Celt's Paradise*, which was praised
by Sir Walter Scott. His verse-tragedy *Damon and Pythias* was staged at
Covent Garden, with Kemble and Macready in the title roles. Early in 1822,
he married and moved to London contributing to the *Literary Register* and
writing librettos for the English Opera House.

With his brother, Banim had planned a series of Irish stories comparable
to Scott's Waverley novels. *Tales by the O'Hara Family* (1825) was an
immediate success; Michael (Barnes O'Hara) had written the first of its three
stories, "Cahoore of the Billhook", John (Abel O'Hara) the other two. John's
long historical novel *The Boyne Water* appeared in 1826, as did the second
Tales; John wrote both of its stories, notably "The Nowlans", a vivid if
melodramatic portrait of a spoiled priest. Michael's novel *The Croppy*,
dealing with the 1798 rising, provided the third *Tales* (1827).

In 1829 continued ill health forced John to seek a better climate in France,
but he was further weakened by cholera in 1832 and was unable to walk when
Michael persuaded him to return to Kilkenny in 1835. After a further
collaboration, *Father Connell* (1840), he died at his home, Windgap Cottage,
on 13 August 1842. Michael Banim was for some years postmaster of Kilkenny
before retiring to Booterstown, Co. Dublin, where he died on 30 August 1874.

The Rothe Museum in Kilkenny has mementoes and a portrait of John
by his friend George Mulvany. The nearby Tholsel has a bust by John Hogan.
The brothers' graves are at St John's Church. Windgap Cottage is on the
Dublin Road.

SAMUEL LOVER

| 1797–1868

Lover, a stockbroker's son, was born in Dublin on 24 February 1797.
He showed an early talent for music and drawing, but at fifteen he was put
to work in his father's office. Lover found the work uncongenial and soon
determined to earn a living as a painter. He left home and within a few years
had gained a reputation for seascapes and particularly miniatures. He was
elected to the Royal Irish Academy in 1828, becoming its secretary in 1830.

His first appearance as a song-writer was in 1818, when he performed at a
banquet in honour of Thomas Moore (*see page 20*), his success providing an
entrée into the best drawing-rooms in Dublin. He was not Moore's equal in
sentimental ballads, and Lady Morgan (*see page 19*) advised him to turn to
humorous subjects. "Rory O'More" was immediately popular and set a new
fashion for comic love songs. Lover also wrote such songs as "Molly Carew",
"I'm Not Myself At All" and "Widow Machree".

In 1831 Lover published *Legends and Stories of Ireland*, a collection of
tales he had written for Dublin magazines, with his own etchings. In 1833
he helped to found the *Dublin University Magazine*. He still considered
himself primarily an artist, however, and his reputation spread to England
when his miniature of the violinist Paganini was exhibited at the Royal
Academy in 1833. He then moved to London, becoming a fashionable
miniaturist well regarded in artistic and intellectual circles.

Lover's first novel, *Rory O'More* (1837), was inspired by his popular song,
and he turned it into a play starring the Irish actor Tyrone Power, who also
appeared in his *The White Horse of the Peppers* and *The Happy Man*. His
operetta *The Greek Boy* was staged at Covent Garden, and *Il Paddy Whack
in Italia* at the English Opera House. His best-known comic novel, *Handy
Andy* (1842), featured a blundering servant finally discovered to be an Irish
peer.

When failing eyesight forced Lover to give up painting in 1844, he devised
"Irish evenings", performing his own stories, recitations and songs like "Molly
Bawn" and "The Low-Backed Car". He was so successful that in 1846–8
he undertook a tour of the United States and Canada. Declining health
eventually forced him to seek a better climate in Jersey, and he died at St
Helier's on 6 July 1868.

JAMES CLARENCE MANGAN

1803–1849

Mangan was born in Dublin on 1 May 1803. His father was a grocer, an irascible bully who made his children's lives miserable and who went bankrupt following unwise property speculation. Mangan was apprenticed to a scrivener and later became an attorney's clerk, but he suffered from melancholia and more than once collapsed from overwork. Hallucinations threatened his sanity, and he became a heavy drinker and possibly opium addict. Throughout his life, irregular habits and eccentricities of manner and dress condemned him to poverty.

As a young man, he contributed poems to Dublin journals such as *The Comet* and *The Dublin Penny Journal*. Much of his later work appeared in the influential *Dublin University Magazine*, founded in 1833. At school, Mangan had shown ability as a linguist, and many of his best poems were translations from German, which he also taught. There were also verses drawn from Spanish and from Eastern languages, such as Arabic and Persian.

When employed as a copyist by the new Ordnance Survey of Ireland, Mangan had contact with the scholars George Petrie, John O'Donovan and Eugene O'Curry, and became interested in Gaelic culture. Although his own knowledge of Irish was never substantial, he adapted others' translations into free versions of Gaelic poems, such as "The Woman of Three Cows".

Mangan was an early contributor to *The Nation*, whose founders Charles Gavan Duffy and Thomas Davis (*see page 34*) sought unsuccessfully to have his work published in London. In later years Mangan turned increasingly to patriotic verse; in his best-known poem, "Dark Rosaleen", Ireland is seen as a dethroned queen who will be restored with foreign help.

Mangan's *Anthologia Germanica* was published in 1845, and his versions of *The Poets and Poetry of Munster* appeared soon after his death. Other collections of verse and a scrap of autobiography have since been published, but his prose output – including Gothic stories which owe a debt to Charles Robert Maturin (*see page 22*), whose cloaked garb he copied – is now forgotten.

Mangan has been described as the greatest Irish poet before W. B. Yeats (*see page 52*), who admired his work, but he has never commanded a wide audience. He died in a Dublin hospital on 20 June 1849, apparently a victim of the raging cholera epidemic, though starvation may have played a part.

GERALD GRIFFIN

1803–1840

Griffin was born on 12 December 1803 in Limerick, where his father was a brewer. After his parents emigrated to Pennsylvania in 1820, he lived with a doctor brother in nearby Adare. He gained some journalistic experience in Limerick, wrote a tragedy, *Aguire*, which has not survived, and in 1823 went to London. An acquaintance with John Banim (*see page 25*) helped him to get some hack work, but poverty and ill-health forced him back to Co. Limerick in 1827, shortly after he had sold a collection of Irish stories, *Holland-Tide*.

Griffin settled in Pallaskenry and quickly completed *Tales of the Munster Festivals* (1827), but it was his novel *The Collegians* (1829) which secured his reputation. It was based on a celebrated Limerick murder case in which John Scanlon, son of one of the county's leading families, and his boatman were hanged in 1820 for murder. The victim was Ellen Hanley, whose body was washed ashore in Co. Clare. While the novel is often melodramatic, it describes the many layers of Irish society in a fashion not previously attempted, and interestingly contrasts a stable middle-class Catholic family with the dissolute Protestant gentry.

Within a year, Griffin had published two more novels, *The Rivals* and *Tracy's Ambition*, but his religious nature caused him doubts about the moral value of his colourful fiction, and this was reflected in *The Christian Physiologist* (1830), tales dealing with the five senses. Depressed by Ireland's miserable state, he sought a more heroic past, and his antiquarian studies led to a long historical novel, *The Invasion* (1832).

During his years in Pallaskenry, Griffin had fallen in love with a Quaker, Lydia Fisher, while also on warm terms with her husband and children. In 1838 he escaped his hopeless situation by entering the Christian Brothers teaching order. He died of typhus fever at the North Monastery in Cork on 12 June 1840.

Griffin had burned most of his manuscripts, but in 1842 *Talis Qualis, or Tales of the Jury-room* was published, and a once rejected play, *Gisippus*, was staged at Drury Lane. *The Collegians* remained popular through out the nineteenth century and was adapted by Dion Boucicault (*see page 35*) as *The Colleen Bawn* (1860) and by Julius Benedict as the opera *Lily of Killarney* (1862).

FRANCIS MAHONY

1804–1866

Mahony, best known under the pen-name Father Prout, was born in Cork on 31 December 1804. At an early age he determined to become a Jesuit and pursued his vocation in Paris and Rome. He was a brilliant classical scholar, but lacked self-discipline, and his superiors rightly doubted that he was suited to the priesthood, though a critic of the order wrote that Mahony had "the fanaticism, the dissimulation, the intrigue, and the chicanery of a thorough Jesuit".

Mahony returned to Ireland, becoming prefect of studies at Clongowes Wood, the Jesuit college in Co. Kildare, but resigned after a drunken escapade. He returned to Italy and, although expelled from the Society of Jesus, managed to be ordained as a priest in 1832.

Back in Cork, Mahony showed devotion to the sick and dying during the 1832 cholera epidemic, but quarrelled with his bishop. He moved to London and began writing for *Fraser's Magazine*, edited by William Maginn from Cork. Its contributors included Southey, Thackeray, Coleridge and Carlyle, but Mahony matched their wit, erudition and consumption of wine. He described himself as "Irish potato seasoned with Attic salt".

Mahony took the genuine name of Father Prout, the lately deceased parish priest of Watergrasshill, Co. Cork, but described him as the son of Dean Swift (*see page 6*) and his Stella, a "combination of Socrates and Sancho Panza". The priest's supposed works provided a witty and learned commentary on everything from "Father Prout's Apology for Lent" to "The Rogueries of Tom Moore" (*see page 20*). Mahony even translated Moore's lyrics into Latin, Greek and Old French so that he could pretend they had been stolen. Daniel O'Connell, nicknamed Dandeleone, was another target of Mahony's cruel pen. The articles were first collected as *The Reliques of Father Prout* (1836), and T*he Final Reliques of Father Prout* appeared in 1876.

In 1837 Mahony moved to *Bentley's Miscellany*, edited by Charles Dickens. He travelled restlessly in Europe and Asia Minor, sending back verses, though none achieved the popularity of his earlier poem, "The Bells of Shandon", by which he is best remembered. In 1846 Mahony became Rome correspondent for the *Daily News*, edited by Dickens, and his contributions as Don Jeremy Savanarola were collected as *Facts and Figures from Italy* (1847). He later settled in Paris, where he died on 18 May 1866.

CHARLES LEVER

1806–1872

Lever was born in Dublin on 31 August 1806. The son of an English architect and builder, he studied at Trinity College, Dublin, becoming a bachelor of medicine in 1831. By this time he had travelled in France, Holland and Germany, where he studied medicine at Gottingen, and had also sailed to Quebec as a medical officer on an emigrant ship. Lever had an early reputation as a raconteur and the short-lived *Dublin Literary Gazette* published his "Logbook of a Rambler", describing his experiences on the Continent. He formed a club in Dublin, the Burschenschaft, imitating German student customs in everything but duelling.

In 1832, on the outbreak of a cholera epidemic, the Board of Health despatched Lever to a post in Kilrush, Co. Clare. Later in that year he was appointed to the dispensary in Portstewart, Co. Derry. Lever married soon afterwards and, to augment his modest income, began to submit stories to the *Dublin University Magazine*, founded in 1833. The first instalment of his novel *Harry Lorrequer* (1839) was published in 1837, and with *Charles O'Malley* (1841) did much to ensure the magazine's success. A feature of this and later novels was the illustrations by Phiz, though the caricatures often displeased those who recognised themselves in Lever's descriptions.

Lorrequer is a dashing young English officer whose regiment arrives in Cork, where he enjoys a life of "dining, drinking, dancing, riding, steeple-chasing, pigeon shooting and tandem driving". He is posted to Kilrush and embarks on a series of romantic and other adventures which take him to Paris and Munich before reaching a happy ending. The story is told with gusto and humour, Lever drawing on his own life and on stories heard on his travels, and transmuting real people into memorable characters, such as the rollicking Father Malachy Brennan and the eccentric Arthur O'Leary, always ready with the wrong word in the wrong place.

O'Malley, the hero of Lever's second novel, is a roisterous fellow, whether electioneering in Co. Galway or attending college in Dublin. He is commissioned in the dragoons and serves in the Napoleonic wars, finally seeing Waterloo from the French camp. Lever's military novels are among his best work and also include *Jack Hinton* (1843), with another memorable priest in Father Tom Loftus, and *Tom Burke of "Ours"* (1844).

Lever had meanwhile moved to Brussels, where he soon built up a successful practice. However, in 1842 he returned to Ireland to edit the

Dublin University Magazine. His early work had been published anonymously, but the final instalment of *Jack Hinton* acknowledged his authorship. *Arthur O'Leary* (1844) drew substantially on his travels in Canada and Germany, together with stories of the Napoleonic wars, and some critics rated it his best book. *The O'Donoghue* (1845) dealt with the French expedition to Bantry Bay in 1796.

The novelist Thackeray, who dedicated *The Irish Sketch Book* to Lever, advised the Irish author to move to London. Lever recognised that the editorial chair limited his opportunities to observe the characters and hear the anecdotes on which his best writing depended, but he preferred the Continent. He left Ireland in 1845 and eventually settled in Florence in 1847. Among the novels of this period are *The Martins of Cro' Martin* (1847), mainly set in Connemara and depicting the evils of absentee landlordism and of cholera; *The Knight of Gwynne* (1847), dealing with events leading to the Act of Union; and *Con Cregan* (1854), described as the 'Irish *Gil Blas*'.

In 1858 Lever was appointed British consul in Spezzia, and from 1867 held a similar post in Trieste, where he died on 1 June 1872. Neither post interfered with Lever's writing, but the novels written during this period are not among his best, with the exception of his last, *Lord Kilgobbin* (1872). Lever was often in debt through gambling and extravagance and sometimes published anonymously to obviate the charge of writing too hurriedly. He replied to one query, "You ask me how I write. My reply is, just as I live – from hand to mouth".

SIR SAMUEL FERGUSON

| 1810–1886

Ferguson was born in Belfast on 10 March 1810. Educated at Trinity College, Dublin, he was called to the Irish Bar in 1838. In 1848 he married Mary Guinness, a member of the brewing family, and they entertained Dublin's intelligentsia at their home in North Great George's Street. In 1867 Ferguson gave up law to become deputy keeper of the public records of Ireland, receiving a knighthood for his work in 1878. He became president of the Royal Irish Academy in 1882 and died at Howth, Co. Dublin, on 9 August 1886.

His poems were first published in the short-lived *Ulster Magazine* in 1830, but he reached a wider audience with "The Forging of the Anchor" (1832) in Blackwood's Magazine and contributed both prose and verse to the Scottish journal. "Father Tom and the Pope" was a notable satire on Catholic education. When the *Dublin University Magazine* was launched in 1833 he contributed poems such as "The Fairy Thorn" (1834) and historical tales entitled "Hibernian Nights' Entertainments".

As a barrister, Ferguson at first had little time for writing, but he helped the musician Edward Bunting with his third volume of *The Ancient Music of Ireland* (1840). An interest in the past was encouraged by the poet James Clarence Mangan (*see page 27*) and the scholars John O'Donovan and George Petrie, and Irish mythology inspired poems such as "The Tain Quest" and "The Death of Dermid", which were included in *Lays of the Western Gael* (1865). The collection was more notable, however for his verse renderings of poems and songs translated from the Irish language. Other verse was to appear in *Congal* (1872), an epic poem, *Poems* (1880), and the posthumous *Lays of the Red Branch* (1897).

Ferguson had been a unionist in younger days, but he founded the Protestant Repeal Association in 1848 and successfully defended Richard D'Alton Williams, a fellow poet, against a charge of treason. He wrote a notable "Lament for Thomas Davis" (*see page 34*), while in 1882 the murder of the chief secretary and the under-secretary in Phoenix Park, Dublin, inspired "At the Polo-Ground". W. B. Yeats (*see page 52*) described Ferguson as "the greatest poet Ireland has produced", but today he is most often recalled in love songs such as "The Coolun" and "The Lark in the Clear Air".

SHERIDAN LE FANU

| 1814–1873

Le Fanu was born in Dublin on 28 August 1814. A grand nephew of Richard Brinsley Sheridan (*see page 14*), he was educated at Trinity College, Dublin. He was called to the Irish Bar in 1839, but preferred a career in journalism, eventually amalgamating three newspapers into the *Dublin Evening Mail*, over which he presided until his death. He also became editor and propriet or of the *Dublin University Magazine* in 1861. Le Fanu married in 1844, but on his wife's death in 1858 became increasingly reclusive.

His earliest work appeared in the *Dublin University Magazine*, a series of Irish stories (1838–40) later collected as *The Purcell Papers* (1880). He also wrote the popular ballads "Phaudrig Crohoore" and "Shamus O'Brien", the latter regularly recited by Samuel Lover (*see page 26*) during his tours. His first historical novels, *The Cock and Anchor* (1845) and *Torlogh O'Brien* (1847) published anonymously, were received with indifference.

Le Fanu had published *Ghost Stories and Tales of Mystery* in 1851, and following his wife's death the grieving author became increasingly preoccupied with death and the supernatural. He mostly wrote in bed, between midnight and dawn, and eventually was so seldom seen that friends called him "the Invisible Prince".

A prolific period as novelist began with *The House by the Church-yard* (1863), set in Chapelizod near his first home in Phoenix Park. It is a masterly eighteenth-century tale of murder and miscarriage of justice and, like most of his later novels, it was first serialised in the *Dublin University Magazine*. Thereafter, Le Fanu turned to the Victorian period and in 1864 published both *Wylder's Hand*, another mystery, and his best-known Gothic novel, *Uncle Silas*, in which a guardian plots to murder his niece for her fortune. Silas Ruthyn is the most striking of Le Fanu's many villains and has since appeared in stage adaptations and in a 1947 film.

The best of his other novels are *Guy Deverell* (1865) and *Checkmate* (1870). *In a Glass Darkly* (1872) is an interesting collection of stories linked by Dr Hesselius, a student of psychiatry and the occult; among them is "Carmilla", a story of vampirism which Bram Stoker (*see page 40*) read as a young man. Le Fanu's last novel *Willing to Die*, was completed a few days before his death in Dublin on 7 February 1873.

THOMAS DAVIS

1814–1845

Davis was born in Mallow, Co. Cork, on 14 October 1814. His father, an English army surgeon, had died a month earlier, and Davis was only four when his Irish mother took her four children to live in Dublin. He graduated from Trinity College, Dublin, in 1836 and was called to the Irish Bar a year later. He spent some time in England and on the Continent, studying languages and assembling a library. An 1837 pamphlet on reform of the House of Lords gave no warning that he would soon embrace Irish nationalism. In 1840 Davis became auditor of TCD's historical society and made a notable speech calling for Irish historical studies, reminding his audience, "Gentlemen, you have a country." The speech was published, and Davis began to write scholarly historical and literary articles for *The Citizen*, a monthly periodical, and more topical essays for the daily *Morning Register*. He joined Daniel O'Connell's Repeal Association in 1841, but their alliance was short-lived. Davis deplored O'Connell's acceptance of a ban on a proposed mass rally in 1843 and sought the non-denominational education which O'Connell considered as "godless".

In 1841 Davis and his friend John Blake Dillon met Charles Gavan Duffy, a Catholic journalist and aspiring lawyer from Monaghan. In 1842 the three men launched *The Nation*, seeking (in Davis's words) a union embracing "Protestant, Catholic and Dissenter – Milesian and Cromwellian – the Irishman of a hundred generations and the stranger who is within our gates". Duffy, recognising the power of patriotic verse, encouraged Davis to write poetry for the first time, and he soon found an appreciative audience for poems such as "Lament for Owen Roe O'Neill", "Fontenoy", "The West's Asleep" and "A Nation Once Again". The journal's best ballads were collected as *The Spirit of the Nation* (1843).

Davis was an accomplished journalist, writing as confidently on literature and music as he did on political themes. He planned a monthly series of shilling volumes, *The Library of Ireland* (1845–7), in which his own *Literary and Historical Essays* and *Poems* (1846) proved an inspiration to later nationalists. He and his closest colleagues became known as Young Irelanders, and some were involved in an abortive rising in 1848. By then, however, Davis was dead, having succumbed to fever in Dublin on 16 September 1845.

DION BOUCICAULT

1820–1890

Dionysius Lardner Boursiquot was born in Dublin, probably on 27 December 1820. His mother was married to a much older wine merchant, and Boucicault (as he became) was probably fathered by their lodger, Dr Dionysius Lardner. When Lardner moved to London in 1827, mother and son soon followed. As a schoolboy Boucicault wrote *Napoleon's Old Guard* (1836), and in 1838 adopted the name Lee Moreton, setting off to become an actor.

Within weeks he had played Iago in Gloucester and Hamlet in Cheltenham, and in 1839 his one-act farce *Lodgings to Let* was staged in Bristol and London. His first hit was *London Assurance* (1841) at Covent Garden, billed as "modern" but in the style of Restoration comedy. Five plays were staged in 1842: *The Irish Heiress, A Lover by Proxy, Alma Mater, Curiosities of Literature* and *The Bastille*. Usually harried by creditors, Boucicault wrote prolifically, suggesting that his tombstone should bear the epitaph: "His first holiday". He was briefly married to a wealthy Frenchwoman; it was rumoured that he pushed her to her death in the Alps.

In 1853 Boucicault and the actress Agnes Robertson moved to New York, where they married. His first American hit was *The Poor of New York* (1857), a melodrama remarkable for a fire engine dousing a blaze in the last act. He wrote several plays on contemporary subjects, notably *Jessie Brown, or the Relief of Lucknow* (1858) and *The Octoroon* (1859) on slavery. His next great success was *The Colleen Bawn* (1860), drawn from Gerald Griffin's novel *The Collegians* (see page 28). In Boucicault's adaptation, the wily Myles na Coppaleen becomes a major character, rescuing the heroine and providing the author with a role he still acted in his sixties. Although accused of creating unreal stage Irish characters, Boucicault found further success with *Arrah-na Pogue* (1864) and *The Shaughraun* (1874), in which he played the title role of Conn, "the soul of every fair, the life of every funeral". He continued to contrive spectacles, such as the express train in *After Dark* (1868) and the university boat race in *Formosa* (1869). Boucicault spent his last years teaching acting in New York, where he died on 18 September 1890. By then he was out of fashion, but plays such as *London Assurance* and *The Shaughraun* have been successfully revived in recent years.

WILLIAM ALLINGHAM

1824–1889

Allingham was born in Ballyshannon, Co. Donegal, on 19 March 1824. His father was a bank manager, and in 1838 Allingham reluctantly went to work in the bank. From 1843 he was a regular visitor to London, becoming friendly with Leigh Hunt, Thomas Carlyle, Lord Tennyson and other men of letters. In 1846 he entered the Customs Service, eventually transferring to Lymington, Hampshire, in 1863. He resigned in 1870 to join *Fraser's Magazine* and in 1874 succeeded the historian J. A. Froude as editor.

His first volume of *Poems* was published in 1850, followed by *Day and Night Songs* (1854), which was re-issued in 1855 with woodcuts by Rossetti and Millais and a new title poem, "The Music Master". This melodramatic tale of parted lovers appealed greatly to Victorian sentimentality, but its real merit lies in descriptive passages drawn from Ballyshannon.

A number of Allingham's broadsheet ballads, written to traditional airs, became very popular in Ireland. He collected ballads sold by street hawkers, and in 1864 edited *The Ballad Book.* He also wrote children's songs, notably "The Fairies" with its familiar "Up the airy mountain, Down the rushy glen".

Allingham's most serious poem is *Laurence Bloomfield in Ireland* (1864), a long narrative account of the struggle between landlords and tenants. Bloomfield is a young landlord disturbed by the poverty around him; he dismisses his rapacious land agent, who is shot dead by Ribbonmen, and successfully sets about improving his estates. The idyllic ending is less convincing than the early descriptions of the impoverished landscape; the Russian novelist Turgenev commented, "I never understood Ireland before", and Gladstone quoted from it at Westminster.

Allingham's later collections include *Fifty Modern Poems* (1865), *Evil May Day* (1882) and *Blackberries* (1884), and towards the end of his life he prepared a six volume edition of his verse. He was also a prose writer of ability and in 1873 published a collection of *Rambles* under the pen-name Patricius Walker.

On leaving the Customs Service, Allingham moved to Chelsea to be near his friend Carlyle, and married Helen Paterson, a water-colour painter. He left *Fraser's* in 1879 moved to Surrey and finally to Hampstead, where he died on 18 November 1889. In 1907 the publication of his diary, edited by his wife and a friend, showed how keenly he had observed his contemporaries and recorded their conversations.

CHARLES J. KICKHAM

| 1828–1882

Kickham's home was in the village of Mullinahone, Co. Tipperary, but he was probably born near Cashel on 9 May 1828. His father was a successful draper, and Kickham was destined for the medical profession until a gunpowder accident severely injured his sight and hearing. As a young man he was sympathetic to the ideas of Thomas Davis (*see page 34*) and *The Nation* but, apart from preparing some pikes, took no effective part in the 1848 Young Irelanders' rising, which petered out ignominiously in nearby Ballingarry.

Kickham later joined the Fenian movement, and in 1863 moved to Dublin as one of the editors of its new journal, *The Irish People*. It was suppressed in 1865, and Kickham was later sentenced to fourteen years' penal servitude for treason felony. He was soon transferred to Woking invalid prison and was pardoned and released in 1869. Despite his disabilities he remained an active Fenian, becoming president of the supreme council of the secret Irish Republican Brotherhood. He died at Blackrock, Co. Dublin, on 22 August 1882.

Kickham's early writings had included poems and ballads, of which "Rory of the Hill" and "Slievenamon" remain popular. His first novel, *Sally Kavanagh, or The Untenanted Graves*, published soon after his release from prison, had been serialised in the *Hibernian Magazine* in 1864. Much of Kickham's journalism was now reprinted in Ireland and America, and he was encouraged to begin a new novel for serialisation in the New York *Emerald*. The *Emerald* soon foundered, but the completed novel found an Irish publisher in 1873.

Knocknagow, or The Homes of Tipperary is a sentimental novel about the destruction of a Tipperary village and reflects Kickham's preoccupation with the evils of landlordism. Its merit lies in the depiction of country scenes and people, at its best recalling the tales of William Carleton (*see page 23*). Incidents such as the sledge-throwing contest between Mat the Thrasher and Captain French, and the death of the consumptive Norah Lahy, appealed to an unsophisticated readership. A new edition appeared in 1879, and for decades *Knocknagow* remained the most widely read novel in Ireland.

Kickham completed two other novels, which were published posthumously: *For the Old Land* (1886) and *The Eagle of Garryroe* (1920), a story of the 1798 rising which had been serialised just before his death.

WILLIAM EDWARD HARTPOLE LECKY

1838–1903

Lecky was born into a wealthy property-owning family at Newtown Park, Co. Dublin, on 26 March 1838. He abandoned early thoughts of taking holy orders and, on graduating from Trinity College, Dublin, travelled widely in Europe, as he was to do throughout his life. His early publications were anonymous and attracted little attention: *Friendship, and Other Poems* (1859), *The Religious Tendencies of the Age* (1860) and *Leaders of Public Opinion in Ireland* (1861).

However his *History of the Rise and Influence of the Spirit of Rationalism in Europe* (1865) brought immediate fame, and the young author found himself much in demand in intellectual circles. The two-volume study traced mankind's gradual discarding of magic and superstition in favour of reason and moral ideas and revealed the breadth of Lecky's reading. Settling in London, Lecky soon completed an equally successful companion piece, *History of European Morals from Augustus to Charlemagne* (1869). In 1870 Queen Sophia of the Netherlands asked to meet the historian during a visit to England, and the following year he married her maid of honour, Elisabeth van Dedem.

In 1878 the first two volumes of Lecky's *History of England in the Eighteenth Century* appeared to acclaim. Much of this great work is devoted to Ireland, where he carried out extensive research. His intent was to counteract the hostile portrait of the Irish in J. A. Froude's *The English in Ireland in the Eighteenth Century*, though his own view of contemporary Ireland was that "the classes who possess political power in Ireland are radically and profoundly unfit for self-government". The final volume was published in 1890 and was followed in 1892 by a cabinet edition separating the English and Irish histories.

Lecky opposed Home Rule in letters and articles in the major journals. Nonetheless, when in l895 he was elected MP for Dublin University, his first speech was on behalf of Fenian prisoners. He supported the creation of a Roman Catholic university in Ireland. Later publications were *Democracy and Liberty* (1896), a discursive work on politics, *The Map of Life* (1899), and a revision of *Leaders* (1903), which was finally accepted as a valuable assessment of Flood, Grattan and O'Connell. Ill-health forced Lecky to resign from parliament in 1902, the year in which he received the Order of Merit, and he died in London on 22 October 1903.

STANDISH O'GRADY

1846–1928

O'Grady was born in Castletown Berehaven, Co. Cork, on 18 September 1846. He was the son of a well-connected Church of Ireland rector, but O'Grady declined holy orders and, on graduating from Trinity College Dublin, in 1868 opted to become a barrister. He began to research his country's heroic past at the Royal Irish Academy, finding a rich body of history and mythology which his earlier education had ignored. At his own expense O'Grady published his *History of Ireland*, comprising *The Heroic Period* (1878) and *Cuculain and his Contemporaries* (1880). The two volumes retold legends concerning the Tuatha De Danann (Ireland's early gods), the Ulster warriors of the Red Branch and the Fianna (led by Finn MacCool). O'Grady had to rely on translations of the confused and contradictory fragments of the legends, and his own imaginative versions were adapted to the prudish sensibilities of the Victorian age.

History of Ireland: Critical and Philosophical (1881) took a more rigorous view of his sources, but O'Grady's works generally reveal a conflict between scholar and romanticist. It was intended as the first volume in a comprehensive history, but O'Grady turned his researches in the Tudor period into a novel, *Red Hugh's Captivity* (1889) – revised as *The Flight of the Eagle* (1897)– a play *Hugh Roe O'Donnell* (1902), and the short stories of *The Bog of Stars* (1893). The hero of *Ulrick the Ready* (1896) is a fictional character, but O'Grady stresses the accuracy of his portrayal of the 1601 battle of Kinsale. In search of a wider audience, O'Grady also published a trilogy of novels: *The Coming of Cuculain* (1894), *In the Gates of the North* (1901) and *The Triumph and Passing of Cuculain* (1920).

Despite their shortcomings, O'Grady's works were important in leading W. B. Yeats, George Russell (*see pages 52 & 55*) and others towards Irish mythology. Russell called him "the last champion of the Irish aristocracy", and in *The Crisis in Ireland* (1882) and *Toryism and Tory Democracy* (1886) O'Grady tried to persuade his own landlord class to develop new industries and employment. The *All Ireland Review*, which he founded in 1900, provided an outlet for his views for several years but he then gave up political activity. He left Ireland for health reasons in 1918 and died on the Isle of Wight on 18 May 1928.

BRAM STOKER

| 1847–1912

Abraham Stoker was born in Dublin on 8 November 1847. On leaving Trinity College, Dublin, he joined the civil service, but his principal interest was the theatre, and in 1871 he became an unpaid drama critic of the *Dublin Evening Mail*. In 1876 an admiring review of Henry Irving's *Hamlet* at the Theatre Royal in Dublin led to an invitation to meet the famous actor. It was the beginning of a warm friendship, and in 1878, when Irving took over the Lyceum Theatre in London, he asked Stoker to become his business manager. The partnership lasted until Irving's death in 1905.

In 1882 Stoker published a collection of children's stories, *Under the Sunset*, in which his taste for the macabre was apparent; one story is drawn from his mother's memory of a cholera outbreak in Sligo. His first novel, *The Snake's Pass* (1890), concerns a search for legendary treasure in the West of Ireland, and he went on to write *The Shoulder of Shasta* (1895) and *The Watter's Mou* (1895) before publishing his famous novel *Dracula* in 1897. While Stoker drew the name from Vlad Dracula, a fifteenth-century Wallachian prince given to impaling his enemies on stakes, there had been earlier works on vampirism, notably a story by his compatriot Sheridan Le Fanu (*see page 33*). Stoker had not visited Transylvania but considerable research in the British Museum allowed him to furnish a convincing setting for Count Dracula's castle. *Dracula* was generally well received by reviewers, who drew comparisons with such novels as *Frankenstein* and *The Fall of the House of Usher*. However, it was Hamilton Deane's 1924 dramatisation of the novel, long after Stoker's death, that made the character of Dracula famous, leading eventually to a notable 1931 film starring Bela Lugosi, who had played the role on Broadway. New adaptations continue to be made for stage and screen.

Stoker's later novels, romances as well as his more effective horror stories, include *Miss Betty* (1898), *The Jewel of the Seven Stars* (1903), *The Lady of the Shroud* (1909) and *The Lair of the White Worm* (1911). He also wrote his *Personal Reminiscences of Henry Irving* (1906) and *Famous Impostors* (1910). Stoker died in London on 20 April 1912. *Dracula's Guest, and Other Weird Stories*, containing some of his best works of horror, was published in 1914.

40

GEORGE MOORE

1852–1933

Moore was born at Moore Hall, Ballyglass, Co. Mayo, on 24 February 1852. The house had been built by the novelist's great-grandfather, a wine merchant who married into a Spanish Catholic family; his son John Moore was briefly proclaimed president of the republic of Connaught during the 1798 French invasion and died in prison. Moore himself was educated at a Roman Catholic school near Birmingham, but he loathed it and later rejected Catholicism.

Moore's father was elected to parliament in 1868 and took the family to London. An army career was planned for Moore, but his father died in 1870, and at twenty-one he left for Paris to fulfil an ambition to become an artist. In the next few years he mixed with painters such as Renoir, Degas, Monet and, returning briefly to London, Whistler and Millais. Recognising his own inadequacy as a painter, he turned to writing, publishing two early volumes of poetry, *Flowers of Passion* (1878) and *Pagan Poems* (1881).

In 1880 the land war and the withholding of rents forced Moore to return to Ireland. He put affairs at Moore Hall in order as best he could, then moved to London, finding journalistic work as he completed his first novel. In France Moore had been converted to the new naturalist movement in literature and had met Émile Zola in Paris. The French author's influence is certainly apparent in *A Modern Lover* (1883), which recounts the experiences of a rising young artist in London, and of the women he betrays in pursuit of success.

Moore joined a touring company to acquire the right naturalistic atmosphere for *A Mummer's Life* (1885), in which a strolling player rescues a draper's wife from her dull existence. Similarly, he took part in the Dublin season to acquire material for *A Drama in Muslin* (1886), a sharply satirical portrait of Anglo-Irish society. As in other novels, Moore writes understandingly of women (there is no hero) and paints a notable portrait of a "new woman", Alice Barton.

Moore gradually moved away from Zola's naturalism, seeking to describe not merely observed events but the psychological milieu in which they occurred. His later influences were the aesthete Walter Pater, Ivan Turgenev and the French writer Edouard Dujardin, who had made use of the interior monologue in *Les Lauriers Sont Coupés*. However, while there was a good reception for *Confessions of a Young Man* (1888) and the essays of *Impressions and Opinions* (1891) and *Modern Painting* (1893), there were several failures before his first major work, *Esther Waters* (1894). Esther is a servant girl, and in the naturalist tradition she might have succumbed to her oppressive environment. Instead, she rebels against it. Forced into service she becomes pregnant by another servant who abandons her; she leaves her child with a farmer, then rescues it. Her subsequent life is hard, but she maintains her own integrity and concludes, "There's a good time coming; that's what I always says".

The short stories of *Celibates* (1895) were followed by two more novels, *Evelyn Innes* (1898) and *Sister Teresa* (1901), but Moore was unhappy with his work. In 1901 he settled in Dublin, joining his friends W. B. Yeats (*see page 52*) and Edward Martyn as a director of the Irish Literary Theatre, but his propensity for petty quarrels was well exercised in the following decade. He published a new collection of Irish stories, *The Untilled Field* (1903), and a short novel, *The Lake* (1905), before returning to London in 1911. His acerbic account of these Irish years, *Hail and Farewell*, appeared in three parts, *Ave, Salve* and *Vale* (1911–14), settling old scores with cruel descriptions of Yeats and others. Moore, ever prolific, wrote with increasing elegance. Of his later novels, *The Brook Kerith* (1916) and *Heloise and Abelard* (1921) are the most notable, while *Conversations in Ebury Street* (1924) contains challenging literary judgements. He was out of fashion when he died in London on 21 January 1933, and not until recent years has his whole body of work begun to receive renewed attention.

LADY GREGORY

1852–1932

Augusta Persse was born at Roxborough House, near Loughrea, Co. Galway, on 15 March 1852. In 1880 she married Sir William Gregory of nearby Coole Park, a retired governor of Ceylon. He was thirty-five years older and died in 1892. Gregory's *Autobiography* (1894) was edited by his widow, who also compiled *Mr Gregory's Letter Box* (1898) from his grandfather's correspondence as Irish under-secretary. During her marriage Lady Gregory had become an active pamphleteer, writing on such subjects as cottage industries in the West of Ireland and the 1886 Home Rule Bill. Her researches converted her to Home Rule, and meetings with W. B. Yeats (*see page 52*) led to a plan for an Irish national theatre.

Yeats's *The Countess Cathleen* (1899) was the first production of the Irish Literary Theatre in Dublin, and in 1904 the Abbey Theatre opened with his *On Baile's Strand* and her comedy *Spreading the News*. Her unexpected gift for comedy was further displayed in one-acters, such as *The Rising of the Moon* (1907) and *The Workhouse Ward* (1908), which remain popular. She also wrote folk history plays, such as *Kincora* (1905) and *Dervorgilla* (1907). She remained a director of the Abbey until her death and did much to foster the work of Seán O'Casey (*see page 67*).

Most of Lady Gregory's plays use a stage Irish dialect, named Kiltartan from the village near her home, employing grammatical constructions drawn from the native language. Several Molière plays were translated into Kiltartan, including *The Doctor in Spite of Himself* (1906) and *The Miser* (1909). She formed a local branch of the Gaelic League and translated Irish sagas in *Cuchulain of Muirthemne* (1902) and *Gods and Fighting Men* (1904). She also published several collections of the folk tales she gathered avidly, most notably *Visions and Beliefs in the West of Ireland* (1920). During the War of Independence her articles in the English weekly *The Nation* were outspoken in criticising the Black and Tans.

Today Lady Gregory is most remembered as an influential figure in the Irish Literary Revival, whose major figures gathered regularly at Coole. Her valuable account of *Our Irish Theatre* (1914) was followed by the posthumous publication of *Lady Gregory's Journals* 1916–30 (1946), edited by Lennox Robinson (*see page 74*), and her autobiographical *Seventy Years* (1974). She died at Coole on 22 May 1932.

Kiltartan has a Gregory museum.

PERCY FRENCH

1854–1920

French was born in Cloonyquin, Co. Roscommon on 1 May 1854. His family were Anglo-Irish gentry and he enjoyed a sheltered "big house" childhood. He entered Trinity College, Dublin, in 1872, but some years passed before he graduated as a civil engineer, for he showed a preference for "the banjo, lawn tennis and water-colour painting instead of chemistry, geology and the theory of strains". His first popular song, "Abdallah Bulbul Ameer" was written in 1877 for a TCD smoking-concert, but his failure to copyright it denied him royalties, and a pirated version quickly appeared in London.

In 1881 French was appointed to the Board of Works in Co. Cavan, and as an inspector of drains bicycled throughout the county. His rural encounters inspired songs such as "Phil the Fluter's Ball" and "Slattery's Mounted Fut". Sacked during an economy drive, French became editor of *The Jarvey*, a new comic magazine on the lines of *Punch*, but it folded soon after its appearance in 1889. In 1891 he collaborated with William Houston Collisson, a well-known Dublin pianist and arranger, on a musical, *The Knight of the Road,* followed in1892 by *Strongbow*.

Meanwhile, his young wife had died in childbirth, and French decided to make a living as a performer. He and two friends had put on an entertainment called *Dublin Up-to-Date*, with songs, recitations and lightning sketches drawn by French and William Orpen, later a famous artist. He now turned this into a one-man show which he toured profitably throughout Ireland. His collaboration with Collisson continued, notably in a new show, *Midsummer Madness* (1893).

In 1894 French married an English actress who had appeared in *Strongbow*, and successful tours outside Ireland persuaded him to move to London in 1906. His water-colours also became popular, and he held regular exhibitions there. Annual tours in Ireland continued to draw large audiences and provided many opportunities for painting.

Sentimental and comic songs flowed readily from French's pen, notably "The Mountains of Mourne", "Eileen Oge" and "Come Back, Paddy Reilly". "Are Ye Right There, Michael?" was inspired by the unreliable narrow gauge line of the West Clare Railway Company, which he successfully sued when a breakdown made him miss a concert. French was returning from a Scottish tour when he took ill and died at Formby, Lancashire, on 24 January 1920.

OSCAR WILDE

1854–1900

Oscar Fingal O'Flahertie Wills Wilde was born in Dublin on 16 October 1854. His father, Sir William Wilde, was a successful eye and ear specialist, an antiquarian and the author of a book on the last days of Jonathan Swift (*see page 6*). His mother, niece of Charles Robert Maturin (*see page 22*) and a convert to Irish nationalism, contributed articles and verse to *The Nation* under the pen-name Speranza. In a famous court case, she was sued for libel when she wrote an indiscreet letter about one of her husband's many mistresses.

As a child Wilde was allowed to frequent his mother's salon, which attracted authors such as Sheridan Le Fanu (*see page 33*) and the Greek scholar John Pentland Mahaffy. Mahaffy, whom Oliver St John Gogarty (*see page 62*) thought "the finest talker in Europe", became Wilde's mentor at Trinity College, Dublin.

In 1874 Wilde won a scholarship to Magdalen College, Oxford, graduating four years later. He visited Italy and Greece with Mahaffy in 1877, and in the following year won the Newdigate prize with his poem "Ravenna". At Oxford Wilde was much influenced by John Ruskin, Walter Pater and John Henry Newman, but resisted the temptation to follow Newman into the Catholic Church. He became an advocate of aestheticism, announcing his pursuit of "beauty for beauty's sake" by symbolic eccentricities, such as peacocks' feathers, sunflowers, blue china, long hair and velveteen breeches.

In 1879 Wilde moved to London, where his wit soon made him a familiar figure in London's drawing-rooms. He was regularly caricatured in *Punch* and was satirised in Gilbert and Sullivan's comic opera *Patience*. In 1882 he embarked on a lecture tour in America, advising a New York customs officer that he had nothing to declare but his genius. He married Constance Lloyd, daughter of an Irish barrister, in 1884.

Wilde had published a collection of early and derivative *Poems* in 1881 and determined on a literary career. He reviewed books in the *Pall Mall Gazette*, wrote on theatre for *The Dramatic Review* and briefly edited *Woman's World*. His first real success was *The Happy Prince and Other Tales* (1888), a collection of fairy stories with a satirical edge. It was followed by *Lord Arthur Savile's Crime and Other Stories* (1891) and *A House of Pomegranates* (1892). Wilde's only novel, *The Picture of Dorian Gray* (1891), shocked the Victorian public, who found it immoral; the book's ageing epigrammatist and seducer, Lord Harry Wotton, is perhaps a self-portrait.

The scintillating conversations in *The Picture of Dorian Gray* hinted at Wilde's potential as a playwright, and the staging of *Lady Windermere's Fan* (1892) confirmed it. Within a brief period Wilde wrote three more comedies, *A Woman of No Importance* (1893), *An Ideal Husband* (1895) and *The Importance of Being Earnest* (1895), becoming the most popular playwright in London. The earlier plays are now dated but can still give pleasure; the last has few challengers as the finest comedy in the English language. Wilde's only setback was the lord chamberlain's refusal to license *Salomé*, for which Sarah Bernhardt had begun rehearsals in 1891, because it portrayed biblical characters; the play, originally written in French, later became a success in Europe.

Wilde's downfall was sudden. He had formed a liaison with Lord Alfred Douglas, son of the eighth Marquis of Queensberry. When the aggressive Queensberry publicly accused Wilde of sodomy, the playwright charged him with criminal libel. Wilde collapsed under cross-examination by the barrister Edward Carson, a contemporary at TCD, and was immediately charged with homosexual offences. In May 1895 Wilde was sentenced to two years' hard labour, his prison experiences inspiring a long poem, *The Ballad of Reading Gaol* (1905). A long letter to Douglas was eventually published as *De Profundis* (1905).

On his release from prison in 1897, Wilde left for France, where he called himself Sebastian Melmoth, the surname drawn from Maturin's greatest novel. A broken man, he died of cerebral meningitis in Paris on 30 November 1900, a day after he had been received into the Catholic Church.

GEORGE BERNARD SHAW

1856–1950

Shaw, the son of a corn merchant, was born in Dublin on 26 July 1856. His mother was a talented mezzo-soprano whose singing teacher, George Vandeleur Lee, joined the household and provided Shaw with a useful musical education. In 1873 Lee moved to London, and Shaw's mother followed. Shaw had become an estate agency clerk, but he disliked Dublin and joined his mother in 1876.

A small legacy allowed him to develop his writing skills, and he completed five early novels, notably *Love Among the Artists* and *Cashel Byron's Profession*. The latter was serialised in a socialist magazine, but book publishers showed no interest until Shaw became famous. During this period Shaw embraced both socialism and vegetarianism. He joined the Fabian Society in 1884 and formed a close friendship with Sidney and Beatrice Webb. Overcoming his shyness, he became an orator equally effective in Hyde Park or the Albert Hall.

Another friend was the drama critic William Archer, who found journalistic work for Shaw, reviewing books for the *Pall Mall Gazette* and as art critic of *The World*. Archer imbued Shaw with his own enthusiasm for the plays of Henrik Ibsen, and Shaw developed a lecture to the Fabians into *The Quintessence of Ibsen* (1891). He also became an entertaining music critic for *The Star* under the pen-name Corno di Bassetto and wrote on the theatre for the *Saturday Review*.

Shaw's first play was *Widowers' Houses* (1892), a study of landlordism. His second, *The Philanderer*, was not staged until 1907. The lord chamberlain then banned *Mrs Warren's Profession*, which dealt with prostitution; it was not seen in the West End until 1925 However, Shaw had a modest success with the comedy *Arms and the Man* (1894), whose opening night applause was broken by a single dissenting voice. "I quite agree with you," Shaw retorted, "but what can we two do against so many?"

Before the end of the century he had written *Candida, The Man of Destiny, You Never Can Tell, The Devil's Disciple*, an American success in 1897, *Caesar and Cleopatra* and *Captain Brassbound's Conversion*. In 1898 he married Charlotte Payne-Townshend. A wealthy Fabian, she nursed him through serious illness and provided the financial security which allowed Shaw to concentrate on writing plays. They moved to Ayot St Lawrence in Hertfordshire in 1906.

Shaw had offered *John Bull's Other Island* to the Irish Literary Theatre in Dublin in 1904, but W. B. Yeats (*see page 52*) turned it down. Harley Granville-Barker accepted it for the Royal Court Theatre in London, where a run of successes finally established Shaw as a major playwright. Arthur Balfour, the prime minister, saw the play four times; King Edward VII laughed so much he broke his seat. It was followed by *Man and Superman* (1905), *Major Barbara* (1905) and *The Doctor's Dilemma* (1906), in each case with Shaw as producer. *The Shewing-up of Blanco Posnet* (1909) was staged in Dublin after the lord chamberlain had banned it as blasphemous.

Shaw's next great success was *Pygmalion* (1914), which after his death was transmuted into the musical comedy *My Fair Lady*. The play was suspended on the outbreak of World War I, during which Shaw incurred unpopularity with "Common Sense about the War" in the *New Statesman*, suggesting that soldiers of every army might do well to shoot their officers. He criticised the execution of prisoners of war after the 1916 Easter Rising in Dublin and similarly opposed the execution of Roger Casement.

Shaw's post-war successes included *Heartbreak House* (1921) and *Saint Joan* (1923), and he received the Nobel Prize for Literature in 1925. His best work was now over, but *The Apple Cart* (1929) and *Too True to Be Good* (1931) contain typical Shavian argument. He also explored political, economic and religious ideas in books such as *An Intelligent Woman's Guide to Socialism and Capitalism* (1928) and *The Adventures of the Black Girl in her Search for God* (1932). Shaw died at Ayot St Lawrence on 2 November 1950.

A Shaw museum has been opened at his birthplace, 33 Synge Street, Dublin.

E. Œ. SOMERVILLE AND MARTIN ROSS

| 1858–1949 1862–1915

Edith Œnone Somerville was born on 2 May 1858 in Corfu, Greece. Violet Martin, a second cousin, was born near Moycullen, Co. Galway, on 11 June 1862. Somerville's father, an army officer, retired in 1859 to the family home in Castletownshend, Co. Cork. The two women met there in 1886, were immediately drawn to one another and embarked on a literary partnership which endured in name long after one cousin's death.

Somerville had another cousin Violet, so she called her new friend Martin; the latter drew the rest of her pen name from Ross House, her family home. Somerville had studied art in London and Paris and was already in demand as an illustrator. Martin's elder brother Robert was a well-regarded journalist in London, and she hoped to emulate his success. The two women soon agreed to collaborate, and the London *Graphic* published their article on palmistry later in the year. In time, Somerville discovered that her main talent also lay in writing.

Within a year they had embarked on a novel, *An Irish Cousin* (1889). Conceived as a "shocker", it had a melodramatic plot, but the cousins were both products of the "big house" and the book contains knowledgeable descriptions of the idle life of the Anglo-Irish gentry. A second novel, *Naboth's Vineyard*, appeared in 1891.

Meanwhile, the cousins began to write travel articles for magazines, and these led to *Through Connemara in a Governor's Cart* (1892) and *In the Vine Country* (1893). Here and in later collections, such as *Beggars on Horseback* (1895), *All on the Irish Shore* (1903) and *Some Irish Yesterdays* (1906), the tone is usually light hearted.

The cousins' first major achievement was the novel *The Real Charlotte* (1894), a Balzacian portrait of Ascendancy society in the twilight of the Victorian age. Charlotte Mullen is a malign and yet pathetic spinster who manipulates people and events with great success except in matters of the heart. Her passion for the land agent Roddy Lambert is frustrated by her flirtatious cousin Francie Fitzpatrick, whom Lambert marries after Charlotte has contrived his first wife's death. Francie's eventual death only increases Charlotte's tragedy.

The Silver Fox (1897), a slighter novel, was followed by *Some Experiences of an Irish R.M.* (1899), the first of the three collections of comic stories by which Somerville and Ross are best remembered. The stories

49

feature a bemused English magistrate, Major Sinclair Yeates, who finds himself dispensing justice among the sly peasantry of west Cork. The stories draw substantially on the cousins' knowledge of the hunting field. Somerville was master of the West Carberry Hunt for some years – Ross was also a keen horsewoman until a hunting accident in 1898 made her a semi-invalid and probably led to her early death.

The trilogy was completed by *Further Experiences of an Irish R.M.* (1908) and *In Mr. Knox's Country* (1915). The stories enjoyed international success, inducing explosive laughter to the point that they were recommended as a cure for quinsy. Among the memorable characters are Flurry Knox, who looks like "a stableboy among gentlemen and a gentleman among stableboys"; his formidable grandmother, Mrs Knox of Aussolas, "dressed as if she had robbed a scarecrow"; and the magistrate's "valued companion" Slipper, a rogue with "an eye like that of a profligate pug" and usually "slightly advanced in liquor".

The cousins completed one other novel, *Dan Russel the Fox* (1915), before Martin Ross died in Cork on 21 December 1915. Somerville had for some years been interested in spiritualism, and she believed that her cousin continued to collaborate through automatic writing at seances. Consequently, almost all her later writings were published under both names. Among them are the novels *Mount Music* (1919), *An Enthusiast* (1921), *The Big House at Inver* (1925), a fine account of the decline of an Anglo-Irish family and an illegitimate daughter's vain attempt to restore its fortunes, *French Leave* (1928), and *Sarah's Youth* (1932). *An Incorruptible Irishman* (1932) is a biography of Charles Kendal Bushe, a lord chief justice of Ireland and the cousins' shared great-grandfather. Edith Somerville died in Castletownshend on 8 October 1949.

AMANDA McKITTRICK ROS

1860–1939

Anna Margaret McKittrick was born at Drumaness, Co. Down, on 8 December 1860. After training in Dublin, she became a teacher in Larne, Co. Antrim, in 1886. She married Andrew Ross, the local stationmaster, in 1887.

Her first novel, *Irene Iddesleigh*, was published in 1897, and thereafter she was known by her pen-name. The Ros was perhaps an imitation of a more elevated Co. Down family. The Amanda came from the romantic heroine of Regina Maria Roche's *The Children of the Abbey*, which influenced her writing, as did Marie Corelli's *The Sorrows of Satan*, which she read in 1895.

Irene marries an older man, runs away with an earlier admirer, marries bigamously in America and dies an outcast. It is an absurd story, told in elaborately ornamental prose. The book was scathingly reviewed in the *Black and White* magazine by the novelist Barry Pain, who introduced it to his literary friends in London; Ros replied in the preface to *Delina Delaney* (1898) and throughout her life dismissed critics as (among other things) curs, cads, corner boys and clay crabs of corruption.

This second novel tells the story of a Connemara fisherman's daughter wooed by a young lord, then framed for attempted murder by a French governess who dies, is later revealed as a cousin the lord once jilted and whom the lord can identify by the six toes on her foot. Before long, convulsed readers formed Ros societies and held Delina Delaney dinners, entertaining themselves by quoting passages of purple prose.

In 1908 Ros inherited a lime kiln, but an ensuing legal battle forced her to sell. She showed her low opinion of lawyers by blowing a toy trumpet outside the offices of solicitors whom she called "Jamie Jarr" and "Mickey Monkeyface McBlear" in *Poems of Puncture* (1913). A second collection, *Fumes of Formation*, appeared in 1933.

Her husband died in 1917, and she remarried in 1922, moving to her second husband's farm in Co. Down. When he died in 1933, she returned to Larne, where she died on 3 February 1939. In 1926 the Nonesuch Press had published a handsome edition of *Irene Iddesleigh*, encouraging her to work on *Helen Huddleson*, an extraordinary novel featuring such characters as Lord Raspberry, Sir Peter Plum and the Earl of Grape. It was completed by her biographer, Jack Loudan, and published in 1969.

51

W. B. YEATS

1865–1939

William Butler Yeats was born in Sandymount, Dublin on 13 June 1865.
The eldest child of the painter John Butler Yeats, he spent much of his
childhood in London, but there were long holidays with grandparents in Sligo,
and many of his poems were inspired by the surrounding countryside.
The family returned to Ireland in 1880, and in 1884 Yeats entered the
Metropolitan School of Art in Dublin. Influenced by the mysticism of his
fellow student George Russell (*see page 55*), Yeats turned to theosophy,
spiritualism and oriental philosophy. Another early influence was the veteran
Fenian John O'Leary, who introduced him to Irish mythology and nationalist
literature.

After the family returned to London, Yeats edited an anthology of *Poems
and Ballads of Young Ireland* (1887) for a Dublin publisher. When his *Folk
and Fairy Tales of the Irish Peasantry* (1888) was published in London,
he acquired a reputation as a folklorist and poet, moving in the same literary
circles as Oscar Wilde and Bernard Shaw (*see pages 45 & 47*). *Wanderings
of Oisin and Other Poems* was well received in 1889.

Soon afterwards Yeats met Maud Gonne, the daughter of an English colonel
and a fanatical convert to the cause of Irish independence. Together they
founded an Association Irlandaise in Paris, but she rejected his marriage
proposals. Yeats wrote *The Countess Cathleen* for her, but the play was not
performed until 1899. Although nominally a member of the Irish Republican
Brotherhood and active in celebrating the centenary of the 1798 rising, Yeats
increasingly concentrated his efforts on literature. A meeting with Lady
Gregory (*see page 43*) in 1896 led to the formation of the Irish Literary
Theatre. Its first production was *The Countess Cathleen*, which aroused
controversy in Dublin. The play was accused of being theologically unsound,
and a scene in which women barter their souls was called an insult to Irish
womanhood. When Yeats and Lady Gregory formed the Irish National Theatre
Society, Maud Gonne took the title role in his *Cathleen ni Houlihan* (1902).
She symbolised Ireland's struggle for freedom, and Yeats later wondered,
"Did that play of mine send out Certain men the English shot?"

Yeats's *On Baile's Strand* (1904) was performed at the opening of Dublin's
Abbey Theatre, of which he was a director throughout his life. Here, and in
plays such as *Deirdre* (1907) and *The Golden Helmet* (1908), Yeats drew on
Irish mythology. Later plays such as *At the Hawk's Well* (1917) and *The Only*

Jealousy of Emer (1919) showed the influence of Japanese Noh drama.

However, it is on his poems that Yeats's reputation principally rests. They are among the greatest in the English language and were collected in volumes such as *Crossways* (1889), *The Rose* (1893), *The Wind Among the Reeds* (1899), *In the Seven Woods* (1903), *The Green Helmet* (1910), *Responsibilities* (1914), *The Wild Swans at Coole* (1919), *Michael Robartes and the Dancer* (1921), *The Tower* (1928), and *The Winding Stair* (1933).

Here are found poems such as "The Stolen Child", "The Lake Isle of Innisfree", "When You Are Old", "September 1913", "An Irish Airman Foresees His Death", "Easter 1916", and "The Second Coming". Here are lines and phrases that persist in the memory: "Romantic Ireland's dead and gone, It's with O'Leary in the grave"; "All changed, changed utterly: A terrible beauty is born"; "Things fall apart; the centre cannot hold; Mere anarchy is loosed upon the world"; "The light of evening, Lissadell, Great windows, open to the south, Two girls in silk kimonos, both Beautiful, one a gazelle"; "Out of Ireland have we come. Great hatred, little room".

In 1917 Yeats married George Hyde-Lees, an English medium, and returned to Ireland. He served in the Irish Free State Senate, received the Nobel Prize for Literature in 1923 and with Shaw and Russell founded the Irish Academy of Letters in 1932. Declining health forced him to winter abroad, and he died at Cap Martin, on the French Riviera, on 28 January 1939.

Yeats museums are found in Sligo and at his summer home, Thoor Ballylee, near Gort, Co. Galway.

GEORGE A. BIRMINGHAM

| 1865–1950

George A. Birmingham was the pen-name of Canon James Owen Hannay, a clergyman's son born in Belfast on 16 July 1865. He was educated at Haileybury and Trinity College, Dublin, graduating in 1887. On taking holy orders, he served in Delgany, Co. Wicklow, before becoming rector of Westport, Co. Mayo, in 1892. Hannay's early writings, such as *The Spirit and Origin of Christian Monasticism* (1903) and *The Wisdom of the Desert* (1904), were published under his own name. However, he sensibly preferred a pseudonym for novels such as *The Seething Pot* (1905), a satirical look at contemporary Irish politics, and *The Northern Iron* (1907), a vivid account of the 1798 rising in Co. Antrim. It was the much less serious *Spanish Gold* (1908) which brought popular success, and he wrote with equal charm and humour in *The Search Party* (1909), *Lalage's Lovers* (1911), *The Major's Candlesticks* (1929) and many other novels.

General John Regan (1913) was written both as a novel and a play and entertained London theatre-goers with its story of a statue erected to a non-existent Irish hero. When the play was performed in Westport, however, it caused a riot. Hannay's parishioners resented his portrayal of small-town gullibility and boycotted him when his identity was revealed.

Hannay departed for a lecture tour in America and later served as an army chaplain in World War I, writing *A Padre in France* (1918). He returned to a small parish in Co. Kildare, then served as chaplain to the British legation in Budapest – writing *A Wayfarer in Hungary* (1925) – before becoming rector of Mells in Somerset in 1924. In 1934 he moved to a parish in London, where, still writing, he died on 2 February 1950.

Hannay was sometimes maligned in Ireland for taking a Protestant Ascendancy view of events, but he is usually very tolerant in his writings. He dispensed satire even-handedly and with courage; *The Red Hand of Ulster* (1912) made as much fun of Northern rebels at a time of gun-running as *Up the Rebels!* (1919) did of their Southern counterparts in an equally troubled period. The titles of a reflective book, *The Lighter Side of Irish Life* (1911), and of the autobiographical *Pleasant Places* (1934) sum up the general outlook of this prolifically entertaining author.

GEORGE RUSSELL

1867–1935

Russell was born in Lurgan, Co. Armagh, on 10 April 1867, but lived in Dublin from 1878. He attended the Metropolitan School of Art where a fellow student, W. B. Yeats (*see page 52*), introduced him to theosophy. Russell always claimed to have mystical visions which inspired his poetry and paintings, and theosophy – with its belief that exceptional individuals had the gift of divine illumination – provided a welcome rationale for his experiences.

He worked for several years as a draper's clerk, but lived in a community of Dublin theosophists, where he met his future wife, an English psychic. His first volume of poetry, *Homeward: Songs by the Way*, was published in 1894 and was followed by *The Earth Breath and Other Poems* (1897) and *The Divine Vision* (1904), in which he drew on Celtic mythology, finding parallels with Eastern mysticism. His pen-name AE came from a compositor's misreading of 'Æon', the name given by Gnostics to the earliest beings.

The dream-like quality of Russell's poems was apparent also in his paintings of the mystical Celtic world, though he was capable of orthodox landscapes and portraiture. His play *Deirdre* (1902) was an influential contribution to the renaissance of Irish drama. Inevitably though, the variety and volume of his work affected its quality, and he is little read today.

In 1897 Russell found work with the Irish Agricultural Organisation Society, and from 1905 edited its weekly journal, *The Irish Homestead*. It later amalgamated with *The Irish Statesman*, which he edited until 1930. The IAOS journal provided an early outlet for writers like James Stephens and Padraic Colum (*see pages 66 & 70*). Always generous to other writers, Russell was sympathetically treated in the acid memoirs of George Moore (*see page 41*), though Moore wondered how the Celtic gods could speak to a man who knew no Irish.

Russell engaged freely in political controversy. He attacked Dublin employers during the 1913 lockout, warned in 1917 that partitioning industrial North from agricultural South would perpetuate hatred, and during the Civil War appealed to republicans to move "from the physical to the intellectual plane". He developed his broader political philosophies in two fictional fantasies, *The Interpreters* (1922) and *The Avatars* (1933). After Eamon de Valera gained power, Russell decided to retire to England, and he died in Bournemouth on 17 July 1935.

J. M. SYNGE

1871–1909

John Millington Synge was born in Rathfarnham, Dublin, on 16 April 1871. His father, a lawyer who owned estates in Wicklow, died of smallpox in 1872. His mother, the daughter of an evangelical rector from Co. Antrim preached doctrines of sin and damnation to her five children. Synge was asthmatic as a child and was educated at home. He walked a good deal and had an early interest in nature; at fourteen he read Charles Darwin, and within two or three years had renounced Christianity, an experience which isolated him from friends and family.

Synge began to study the violin in 1887, and music and literature became his major preoccupations. On graduating from Trinity College, Dublin, in 1892, and with a romance foundering on his atheism, he set off for Germany to continue his studies. He soon had doubts about a career in music, however, and in 1894 moved to Paris, hoping to teach English while studying at the Sorbonne.

In 1896 Synge met W.B. Yeats (*see page 52*), who with Maud Gonne founded the Association Irlandaise to enlist Irish people living in France to the cause of Irish independence. Synge was sympathetic to Irish nationalism, though never politically active. At that time his writing amounted to little more than a few poems and essays, and Yeats advised him to visit the Aran islands and "express a life that has never found expression".

Synge returned to Ireland in 1897 and some months later was operated on for a growth in his neck, a first sign of the Hodgkinson's disease which would condemn him to an early death. He returned briefly to France, but in May 1898 finally reached the Aran islands. During the following six weeks, and on subsequent annual visits, he studied Irish, listened to story-tellers, took photographs and gathered the raw material for most of his later work. Synge was inspired by the islanders' unremitting struggle against the elements, by their belief in the supernatural and by the poetic simplicity of their speech. He later described his experiences in *The Aran Islands* (1907).

On visiting Lady Gregory (*see page 43*) at Coole Park, Synge took part in discussions on the proposed Irish Literary Theatre. When his one-act play *The Shadow of the Glen* was staged in Dublin in 1903, its portrayal of a loveless rural marriage was castigated as "a slur on Irish womanhood". Though set in Co. Wicklow, it was inspired by a story heard in Aran, as was

56

Riders to the Sea (1904), which concerned a drowning. Both plays were soon staged in London.

The Well of the Saints (1905), a tragedy in which blind beggars are disillusioned when their sight is briefly restored, was among the first plays performed by the Abbey Theatre, of which Synge became a director. Again the Dublin critics were unsympathetic.

Among the cast of *The Well of the Saints* was a young Catholic actress, Molly Allgood, sister of the Abbey star Sara Allgood. Under her stage name of Maire O'Neill she created the role of Pegeen Mike in *Playboy of the Western World* (1907), with her sister as the Widow Quin and W. G. Fay as the frightened fugitive transformed by gullible villagers into a heroic figure. There was an uproar on opening night when the puritanical Dublin audience took offence at a reference to "females standing in their shifts", and organised rioting interrupted subsequent performances. The *Freeman's Journal* called the play a "libel upon Irish peasant men and, worse still, upon Irish girlhood", but Yeats had recognised a comic masterpiece and defended it courageously. Synge was now in love with Molly Allgood, but his health deteriorated rapidly, and their wedding had to be postponed in 1908. He died in Dublin on 24 March 1909. *The Tinker's Wedding*, which Yeats had deemed "dangerous at present" and which is seldom performed, had its first production later in the year in London. *Deirdre of the Sorrows* a dramatisation of Gaelic legend which was uncompleted when Synge died, was staged at the Abbey in 1910 with Molly Allgood in the title role.

LYNN DOYLE

1873–1961

Doyle's real name was Leslie Montgomery. He was born in Downpatrick, Co. Down, on 5 October 1873 and on leaving school joined the Northern Bank Company in Belfast. Some years later, he was transferred to Skerries Co. Dublin, and was branch manager there until his retirement in 1934. He died at Malahide, Co. Dublin, on 13 August 1961. Even in his eighties he continued to write the Ballygullion stories for which he was famous.

The fictitious Ulster village made its first appearance in 1907 in the Dublin magazine *Seanachie*. Montgomery took the name from a Downpatrick street known as The Gullion, and his pen-name began as Lynn C. Doyle, inspired by seeing the words linseed oil in a shop. The first collection of stories, *Ballygullion*, was published in 1908; they are told in thick dialect by Patrick Murphy, the village raconteur whom Doyle introduces as his "sporting associate and occasional client". Doyle wrote prolifically, and later collections bore such titles as *Lobster Salad* (1922), *Dear Ducks* (1925), *Me and Mr Murphy* (1930), *Green Oranges* (1947), *Back to Ballygullion* (1953), and finally *The Ballygullion Bus* (1957).

Doyle mostly found his humour in such rural pursuits as poaching, poteen-distilling, matchmaking and backing horses, but the conflicts of Orange and Green are not ignored, even if his satire is always gentle, and differences are resolved with uncommon tolerance and not a little native cunning. In the earliest story, the newly formed creamery society is threatened by sectarianism, but finishes by decorating its butter with a wreath of shamrocks and orange lilies. They are simple stories, but full of invention and warmth, and peopled with memorable comic figures. As Murphy puts it in one story, "In the end we can always laugh at ourselves when there's nobody killed". Such stories could hardly be written today.

Doyle also wrote several plays, notably *Love and Land* (1913), and novels such as *Mr Wildridge of the Bank* (1916) and *Fiddling Farmer* (1937). He published a collection of essays and sketches, *An Ulster Childhood* (1921), and a travel book, *The Spirit of Ireland* (1935). He was the first Irish writer appointed to the Irish censorship board, but resigned in 1937 after only a few weeks. "It is terribly easy to read only the marked passages", Doyle said, "so hard to wade through the whole book afterwards".

FORREST REID

1875–1947

Reid was born in Belfast on 24 June 1875. His ship owning father had suffered financially in the American Civil War and died when Reid was young. Consequently, Reid grew up in an atmosphere of decaying gentility which often pervades his books. He was apprenticed to the tea trade, but after his mother's death a small inheritance allowed him to study at Cambridge University.

In 1908 he returned to Belfast, where he spent the rest of his life, but he enjoyed the friendship of literary figures such as E. M. Forster, Edwin Muir and Walter de la Mare. He was an admirer of Henry James but James severed their correspondence after Reid dedicated *The Garden God* (1905) to him; the novel dealt with the romantic friendship of two schoolboys. Whereas Forster suppressed his novel of homosexuality, *Maurice*, during his lifetime, Reid disguised the homosexual undertones of his novels within the ancient Greek conception of platonic love between equals and the tutelage of adult over boy.

Boyhood and adolescence were virtually his only subjects, treated with a mixture of realism and romanticism. In the autobiographical *Private Road* (1940) he wrote, "I could get on swimmingly until I reached my King Charles's head – the point where a boy becomes a man". *Apostate* (1926) describes his own early years, in which he rejected Christianity in favour of the pantheistic pagan world portrayed in Greek literature and mythology. Reid is in no sense a regional novelist, but his books contain shrewd observations of Ulster life.

The earlier novels include *The Bracknels* (1911) and *Following Darkness* (1912). The first was rewritten as *Denis Bracknel* (1947), the second as perhaps his best novel, *Peter Waring* (1937), whose hero struggles with the problems of young love, art and religion. He also wrote a notable trilogy, *Uncle Stephen* (1931), *The Retreat* (1936) and *Young Tom* (1944), the last winning the James Tait Black prize. The first has a supernatural theme, but the others (covering Tom Barber's earlier life) also have a typical dream-like quality.

Reid also published studies of W. B. Yeats (1915) (*see page 52*) and Walter de la Mare (1929), and a collection of essays, *Retrospective Adventures* (1941). His *Illustrators of the Sixties* (1928), on Victorian woodcut artists, reflected one of several collecting interests. Unmarried, Reid died at Warrenpoint, Co. Down, on 4 January 1947.

DANIEL CORKERY

| 1878–1964

Corkery was born in Cork on 14 February 1878. He trained as a teacher in Dublin and in 1907 returned to Cork, where he taught for many years in national schools. He also studied art, producing fine water-colours of the region around the River Lee, and joined the Gaelic League, becoming an ardent advocate of the Irish language.

In 1908 Corkery helped to found the Cork Dramatic Society, for which he wrote plays in both languages. Three one-act dramas were published as *The Yellow Bittern and Other Plays* in 1920, when the Abbey Theatre staged the moving title-piece. His first collection of short stories was *A Munster Twilight* (1916). It was followed by *The Hounds of Banba* (1920), *The Stormy Hills* (1929) and *Earth out of Earth* (1939), and together they provide a convincing gallery of narrow and frustrated lives in and around Cork. Corkery's only novel, *The Threshold of Quiet* (1917), occupies similar territory, drawing on Thoreau's maxim that "The mass of men lead lives of quiet desperation".

Corkery was much influenced by the Russian author Turgenev, and in turn he encouraged the writing of two of his pupils, Sean O'Faolain and Frank O'Connor (*see pages 83 & 87*). Unlike them, Corkery remained in Cork, becoming a schools inspector in the Irish language. In 1931 he was appointed professor of English at University College, Cork.

Corkery's academic reputation rests on two polemical works. *The Hidden Ireland* (1924) is a study of the life and poetry of Gaelic Munster in the eighteenth century. It was a response to Anglo-Irish writers such as Maria Edgeworth and W. E. H. Lecky (*see pages 17 & 38*), who in his view misrepresented or ignored an important part of Irish life; some critics have challenged Corkery's judgement of poetry and his grasp of history. *Synge and Anglo-Irish Literature* (1931) proved even more controversial, for Corkery argued that Anglo-Irish writers did not understand the Irish consciousness and could not contribute to a national literature on the Russian model.

Corkery's narrow nationalism and fanatical devotion to Irish may have warped his critical judgement, but they did not diminish the quality of the stories he wrote in English. He retired from UCC in 1947, published *The Fortunes of the Irish Language* in 1954, and died at Passage West, Co. Cork, on 31 December 1964.

LORD DUNSANY

1878–1957

Edward Plunkett, who became the eighteenth Baron Dunsany in 1899, was born in London on 24 July 1878. Educated at Eton, he entered the Coldstream Guards in 1899 and served in the Boer War before settling at Dunsany Castle in Co. Meath, which his family had occupied since 1190. The versatile peer was an accomplished cricketer, a chess champion, a big game hunter and, unlike many Anglo-Irish writers, always a devoted servant of the Crown.

In 1905 Dunsany published his first book of stories *The Gods of Pegana*, quickly followed by *Time and the Gods* (1906) and *The Sword of Welleran* (1908). Most were fantasies, not unlike the later work of J. R. R. Tolkien, and he formed an enduring partnership with their illustrator S. H. Sime.

Through his uncle Horace Plunkett, the pioneer of cooperation, Dunsany met W. B. Yeats (*see page 52*) and wrote *The Glittering Gate* (1909) for the Abbey Theatre. *King Argimenes and the Unknown Warrior* (1911) was also produced there, but relations with Yeats and Lady Gregory (*see page 43*) soon deteriorated. Dunsany felt that Lady Gregory had plagiarised *Argimenes* in *The Deliverer*, staged a week earlier, and Oliver St John Gogarty (*see page 62*) reckoned that Yeats envied Dunsany's title.

In 1911 *The Gods of the Mountain* was staged in London; the short play, set in the East, concerns beggars who unwisely pass themselves off as gods. Dunsany's reputation was further enhanced by *The Book of Wonder* (1912), largely inspired by Sime drawings, and several short plays became popular, especially in America. With the outbreak of war in 1914, he became a captain in the Royal Inniskilling Fusiliers; he was on leave in Ireland during the 1916 rising and was wounded after offering his services in Dublin.

Dunsany scored a London hit in 1921 with a full length play, *If*, another Eastern fantasy, then turned to novels such as *The Chronicles of Rodrigues* (1922) and *The Blessings of Pan* (1927). He eventually tackled Irish themes, notably in *The Curse of the Wise Woman* (1933), his most autobiographical novel, and *Up in the Hills* (1935). His African adventures led to the comic figure of Joseph Jorkens, who tells tall stories in the mythical Billiards Club; five Jorkens collections were published between 1931 and 1954. Dunsany died in Dublin on 25 October 1957.

OLIVER ST JOHN GOGARTY

| 1878–1957

Gogarty was born in Dublin on 17 August 1878. While studying at Trinity College, Dublin, he won the vice-chancellor's verse prize three times and was an Irish cycling champion. When he revived the ancient Tailteann Games in 1924, he came third in archery. He was a founder of the Irish Aero Club in 1928. Although it was said that he excelled in everything but medicine, he soon became a successful surgeon.

An early influence was Ireland's other great all-rounder, John Pentland Mahaffy of TCD. Like Mahaffy, Gogarty became a mordant wit, and his scabrous limericks and bawdy ballads circulated throughout Dublin. Later he presided over a convivial group in the Bailey restaurant, who would "sacrifice their mother for a witty phrase". However, when James Joyce (*see page 71*) portrayed him as "stately, plump Buck Mulligan" in *Ulysses*, a furious Gogarty called it "a book you can read on all the lavatory walls in Dublin".

As a doctor, Gogarty had criticised Dublin's slums, and in *Blighty* (1917) dramatised his concerns; antedating Seán O'Casey (*see page 67*), it was the first Abbey Theatre play to discover the poetic language of Dublin's poor. *A Serious Thing* (1919) satirised British rule in Ireland through a portrayal of Romans in the Holy Land.

Gogarty provided a safe house for Michael Collins during the War of Independence and became an Irish Free State senator. Arthur Griffith, the Sinn Féin leader, had hoped his friend Gogarty might become governor-general; after Tim Healy was appointed, Gogarty called the vice-regal lodge "Uncle Tim's cabin".

Kidnapped by republicans in 1923, he escaped by jumping into the River Liffey, to which he later made a gift of swans. His collection of verse, An *Offering of Swans* (1923), was followed by *Wild Apples* (1928), *Others to Adorn* (1938) and *Elbow Room* (1939). W.B. Yeats (*see page 52*) described Gogarty as "one of the great lyric poets of our age".

Gogarty's memoirs include *As I Was Going Down Sackville Street* (1937), *Tumbling in the Hay* (1939) and *It Isn't This Time of Year at All* (1954). After the first led to a libel action, which he lost, he moved to London and then New York, where he published the novels *Going Native* (1940), *Mad Grandeur* (1941) and *Mr Petunia* (1945). He died in New York on 22 September 1957.

MAURICE WALSH

1879–1964

Walsh was born on a farm near Listowel, Co. Kerry, on 21 April 1879.
On joining the Customs and Excise Service in 1901, he was posted to
Limerick, but the largest part of his career was spent in Scotland, particularly
in the Highlands around Speyside and the Moray Firth, where he became
an expert on Scotch whisky. A close friend and colleague was Neil Gunn,
who was also to become a successful novelist.

In 1922 Walsh chose to become an excise officer under the new Irish Free
State. The Civil War had begun and Dublin was a dangerous city at night, so
he devoted his spare time to writing and had some stories accepted by the
Dublin Magazine. In 1925 *The Key Above the Door*, a novel drawing on
experiences in Moray and Skye, was serialised in *Chambers Journal* before
being issued as a book in 1926. This successful formula was repeated with
While Rivers Run (1928), *The Small Dark Man* (1929) and *Blackcock's
Feather* (1932), the last a revised version of a sixteenth-century historical
novel first serialised in the *Irish Emerald* as early as 1908.

Walsh proved equally adept in Scottish and Irish settings, in comedy
and shrewd observation of national traits, and in past and present times,
becoming Ireland's most popular author. In 1933 the *Saturday Evening Post*
published his short story "The Quiet Man". It was revised in a collection called
Green Rushes (1935), and in 1952 the Irish American director John Ford
turned it into a famous film.

Walsh retired from his post in 1933, having successfully fought a
government attempt to reduce pension entitlements during a time of
economic hardship. He moved to Blackrock, Co. Dublin, acquiring an odd job
man who inspired the stories collected as *Thomasheen James, Man-of-no-
Work* (1941). Later novels included *The Road to Nowhere* (1934), inspired
by Kerry tinkers he had known as a boy, *And No Quarter* (1937), *The Hill Is
Mine* (1940), *The Spanish Lady* (1943) and *Trouble in the Glen* (1950),
which was also filmed. In 1940 the *Saturday Evening Post* published a
defence of Irish neutrality which Walsh had written in collaboration with Sean
O'Faolain (*see page 83*), but he was proud of two sons in the British forces.
He died at Blackrock on 18 February 1964.

ROBERT LYND

| 1879–1949

Lynd was born in Belfast on 20 April 1879. His father was a Presbyterian minister, and both parents came from families with a strong Liberal tradition. Lynd's own radicalism was evident from his youth and he joined the Gaelic League in Belfast. In later years he supported Sinn Féin, and for two years was a London delegate on its national executive.

Lynd graduated from Queen's College, Belfast, in 1899. In 1901 he became a journalist on the *Daily Dispatch* in Manchester, but soon moved to London, where he shared a studio with the artist Paul Henry and freelanced for several years. Lynd joined the *Daily News* in 1908, and in the following year married Sylvia Dryhurst, a young Dubliner he had met at a Gaelic League meeting in London. She was to become a well-known novelist and poet, and their Hampstead home became a rendezvous for writers and artists.

In 1912 Lynd became literary editor of the *Daily News* (which later became the *News Chronicle*), and held this post until 1947. However, his reputation principally rests on his contributions to the *New Statesman*, which was launched in 1913. Lynd's weekly essays, over the initials Y. Y. , covered a wide range of subjects with a witty and often whimsical touch. He quickly showed a facility as an essayist comparable to other masters of that now neglected craft, such as G. K. Chesterton and Hilaire Belloc. Lynd's work was collected regularly under such titles as *It's a Fine World* (1930), *Both Sides of the Road* (1934), *I Tremble to Think* (1936) and *Things One Hears* (1945). A selection of *Essays on Life and Literature* (1951), covering many years, was published posthumously.

Ireland often provided Lynd with an essay subject. He could as easily describe humorous encounters at Galway races as he could write soberly of the paradoxical death of the nationalist Tom Kettle in Flanders. Among his books are *Irish and English* (1908), *Home Life in Ireland* (1909), *Rambles in Ireland* (1912) and *Ireland a Nation* (1919). He campaigned vigorously but unsuccessfully against the death penalty imposed on his friend Roger Casement in 1916. Lynd also wrote *Old and New Masters* (1919), *The Art of Letters* (1920) and *Dr Johnson and Company* (1927), the last an entertaining appraisal of the lexicographer and his circle. He died in Hampstead on 6 October 1949.

JOSEPH CAMPBELL

| 1879–1944

Campbell was born in Belfast on 15 July 1879. His father came from south Armagh, where Campbell spent holidays on the family farm, acquiring a knowledge of Irish language and folklore. Early influences were the archaeologist Francis Joseph Bigger and the poet Padraic Colum (*see page 70*). The poet Ethna Carberry, co-founder of the periodical *Shan Van Vocht*, was a cousin. A sister married Sam Waddell, playwright brother of Helen Waddell (*see page 77*).

In 1904 Campbell wrote the words for airs which the composer Herbert Hughes had collected in Co. Donegal. Among the still popular *Songs of Uladh* are "My Lagan Love" and "The Ninepenny Fidil". He acted with the new Ulster Literary Theatre, but his play *The Little Cowherd of Slainge* was unsuccessful. A volume of verse, *The Garden of the Bees,* was published in 1905.

Moving to Dublin, Campbell published *The Rushlight* (1905). Two of its poems provided titles for subsequent collections, *The Gilly of Christ* (1907) and *The Mountainy Singer* (1909), the latter dealing with such country folk as the goat-dealer and the besom-man. In search of work, the poet moved to London in 1906, teaching and becoming secretary of the Irish Literary Society there. In 1911 he married Nancy Maude, a colonel's daughter who had rejected the unionism of her Anglo-Irish forbears, and they settled in Co. Wicklow.

Campbell taught at Patrick Pearse's school, St Enda's, and became active in the Gaelic League. A folk tragedy, *Judgement* (1912), was ill received at the Abbey Theatre. The lyrical poems in *Irishry* (1913) continued his concern with ordinary folk; but, following the 1916 rising, there is a more sombre note in *Earth of Cualann* (1917). Overall, his poems show influences of Blake, Whitman, Coleridge and Pound, and their fine craftsmanship has been unduly neglected.

Later years were less productive. Seventeen months of internment during the Civil War took their toll, and his marriage broke up in 1924. He moved to New York in 1925, founding a school of Irish studies which was eventually absorbed into Fordham University. In 1939 Campbell returned to his farm in Glencree, Co. Wicklow, and in reduced circumstances made some money from broadcasting. For some years he laboured at a long poem, – "A Vision of Glendalough", which was published posthumously. On 7 June 1944 a neighbour found him dead at his fireside.

JAMES STEPHENS

1880?–1950

Stephens claimed to have been born in Dublin on the same day as James Joyce (*see page 71*), but a more likely date is 9 February 1880. In 1886 he was committed for begging to the Meath Protestant Industrial School for Boys in Blackrock, Co. Dublin. He received a good education there and held a series of clerical jobs in solicitors' offices in Dublin.

His first story, "The Greatest Miracle" (1905), was published by Arthur Griffith in *The United Irishman*, and Stephens became an ardent supporter of Griffith's Sinn Féin movement and of the Gaelic League. A volume of poetry, *Insurrections* (1909), was dedicated to his other mentor, George Russell (*see page 55*).

Russell recommended Stephens's first novel, *The Charwoman's Daughter* (1912), to the London publisher Macmillan after it had been serialised in *The Irish Review*. Its heroine has the fairy tale name of Mary Makebelieve, and her story is an odd mixture of optimistic whimsy and the sombre realities of the slum life experienced by its author.

Stephens's reputation largely rests on his fantasy *The Crock of Gold* (1912). Its characters include the nubile shepherdess Caitilin, a verbose philosopher with a shrewish wife, gods of both classical and Celtic origin, and several leprechauns and policemen. A similar novel, *The Demi-Gods* (1914), was less well received. Stephens took a less respectful view of mythology than, say, Lady Gregory or W. B. Yeats (*see pages 43 & 52*), and if he has a literary heir it is Flann O'Brien (*see page 93*).

Stephens became registrar of the National Gallery of Ireland in 1915, and his experience of the 1916 Easter Rising inspired both a volume of poetry, *Green Branches*, and the precise reportage of *The Insurrection in Dublin* (1916). Prompted to further exploration of Ireland's past, he published a collection of poems drawn from Gaelic verse, *Reincarnations* (1918), and three books drawing more narrowly on mythology than his earlier fantasies had done: *Irish Fairy Tales* (1920), *Deirdre* (1923) and *In the Land of Youth* (1924). Disillusioned with the Irish Free State, Stephens moved to London in 1925, undertaking lecture tours in America. He published further volumes of poetry, *Strict Joy* (1931) and *Kings and Moons* (1939), but became better known as a broadcaster on poetry and poets. He died in London on 26 December 1950.

SEÁN O'CASEY

| 1880–1964

John Casey, as he was christened, was born into a lower middle-class Protestant family in Dublin on 30 March 1880. His father died in 1886, after which the family declined into the poverty that prevailed in Dublin's tenements. O'Casey suffered from painful trachoma which impaired his sight, but became a voracious reader and could recite long passages from the Bible.

On leaving school, O'Casey held a number of jobs, becoming a railway labourer in 1901. In 1911 he joined James Larkin's new Irish Transport and General Workers' Union, writing for *The Irish Worker*, and in 1914 he became secretary of James Connolly's Irish Citizen Army. Politically, O'Casey was more strongly devoted to the causes of the working class (eventually becoming a communist) than to Irish nationalism. However, he also joined the Gaelic League (his playwright's name a variant of the Irish Seán Ó Cathasaigh) and the Irish Republican Brotherhood.

Always tendentious and uncompromising, O'Casey soon resigned from the Citizen Army, and consequently took no part in the Easter Rising, though he was briefly imprisoned. When he published *The Story of the Irish Citizen Army* (1919), it had a hostile reception from those who had risked their lives in 1916.

O'Casey had several plays rejected by the Abbey before heeding the advice of Lady Gregory (*see page 43*) that his gift lay in characterisation. The outcome was *The Shadow of a Gunman*, an unexpected success in 1923. Set in 1920 during the War of Independence, it centres on a poet mistaken for a gunman by the other inhabitants of a Dublin tenement. The exchanges between the poet Donal Davoreen and the pedlar Seamus Shields reflect conflicting ideas within the playwright himself; like so many of O'Casey's male characters, each is a braggart and idler.

Much of the success of *The Shadow of a Gunman* depends on the minor characters and their vividly comic dialogue. *Juno and the Paycock* (1925) boasts an even richer portrait gallery, with the memorable "paycock" Captain Boyle and his sponging crony Joxer Daly. The play is set during the "turrible state of chassis" of the Irish Civil War and revolves round the Boyle family's mistaken hopes of an inheritance. Again the men are braggarts, and courage is found only in the women, most notably Juno Boyle herself, meeting every reverse with stoic faith and finally greeting her son's death with "Sacred Heart o' Jesus, take away our hearts o' stone, and give us hearts o' flesh! Take away this murderin' hate an' give us Thine own eternal love!"

The last of O'Casey's Abbey trilogy, *The Plough and the Stars*, deals with the 1916 rising. It opened on 8 February 1926, and rioting broke out on the fourth night, as the play was condemned as an insult to the revolutionary heroes. Yeats recalled the treatment of J. M. Synge (*see page 56*) and asked, "Is this to be the ever recurring celebration of the arrival of Irish genius?" The play survived as the apex of O'Casey's career, with such memorable characters as Fluther Good, yet another braggart, the loyalist Bessie Burgess, the prostitute Rosie Redmond, and poor Norah Clitheroe, trying to keep her vain husband Jack away from the Citizen Army.

In March 1926 O'Casey went to London to receive the Hawthornden prize for *Juno and the Paycock*. He remained in England, marrying the Irish actress Eileen Carey and eventually moving to Devon in 1938. In 1928 the Abbey rejected *The Silver Tassie*, a play about World War I, and an embittered O'Casey severed his links with the theatre. None of his later plays was without merit, but in shedding naturalism O'Casey merely underlined the fact that he lacked Synge's poetic gifts.

The best of these later plays are *Red Roses for Me* (1943), *Purple Dust* (1945), *Cock-a-Doodle-Dandy* (1949), *The Bishop's Bonfire* (1955) and *The Drums of Father Ned* (1959). O'Casey also published six volumes of semi-fictional autobiography, beginning with *I Knock at the Door* (1939) and ending with *Sunset and Evening Star* (1954). He died at Torquay on 18 September 1964.

GEORGE SHIELS

1881–1949

Shiels was born near Ballymoney, Co. Antrim, on 24 June 1981, but he emigrated to America as a young man. He was working on the construction of the Canadian Pacific Railway in 1913 when an accident confined him to a wheel-chair for the rest of his life. He returned to Ballymoney, where he opened a shipping agency with his brother, and began to write stories based on his experiences abroad. For a time he used the pen-name George Morshiels.

His first play, *Away from the Moss*, was staged by the Ulster Literary Theatre in 1918, and this was followed by *Felix Reid and Bob* (1919) and *The Tame Drudge* (1919). Shiels's work attracted the attention of the Abbey Theatre in Dublin, which staged his one-act comedy *Bedmates* in 1921. His first major success was *Paul Twyning* (1922), and Shiels's continuing popularity with Dublin audiences did much to restore the theatre's fortunes. His plays were equally successful in Belfast's Group Theatre.

Much of Shiels's work can be simply categorised as kitchen comedy, and plays such as *Professor Tim* (1925) and *The Old Broom* (1944) are constantly performed in the amateur theatre. However, despite being confined to a "wee room" in Ballymoney, he was a shrewd observer of the changing world around him. *The New Gossoon* (1930) skilfully recorded the effects of radio, cinema, dance hall and internal combustion engine on traditional rural life.

When he turned to tragedy, as in *The Passing Day* (1936), Shiels could be equally effective. Originally a radio play, it uses a flashback technique to portray the miserly life of a small merchant; Tyrone Guthrie revived the work for the 1951 Festival of Britain. *The Rugged Path* (1940), which had a record-breaking run at the Abbey, and its companion piece *The Summit* (1941) contrast a tyrannical mountainy clan with law-abiding lowland farmers, and question the traditional Irish revulsion towards informers.

Shiels has sometimes been criticised for not tackling Ulster's sectarian problems in his plays. However, even in his comedies he had a shrewd eye for the ungenerous qualities of his neighbours, their narrow-mindedness and in particular their avarice, and these are qualities which perhaps hinder a solution to sectarianism. When success as a playwright enabled Shiels to give up the shipping agency, he moved to Carnlough, Co. Antrim, where he died on 19 September 1949.

PADRAIC COLUM

1881–1972

Colum was born on 8 December 1881 in Longford, where his father was workhouse master. At seventeen he became a clerk in the Irish Railway Clearing House in Dublin, but left in 1904 determined to make a living through writing. His first poems appeared in *The United Irishman*, edited by Arthur Griffith. *The Saxon Shillin'* (1902) won a competition for a play to discourage young Irishmen from joining the British army. Colum acted with the new Irish National Theatre Society, but after his play *Broken Soil* was staged in 1903, he concentrated on writing. He was one of the founders of the Abbey Theatre, where his realistic peasant drama *The Land* (1905) was an early success. *Thomas Muskerry* (1910) was also staged by the Abbey, but thereafter Colum failed to fulfil his early promise as a dramatist.

His first book of verse, *Wild Earth*, appeared in 1907, with lyric poems like "The Plougher", "A Drover" and "An Old Woman of the Roads". He married in 1912, and in 1914 the Colums sailed to America, soon entering New York literary circles. Colum began to write children's stories for the *Sunday Tribune*, which led to a collection, *The King of Ireland's Son* (1916), followed over the years by the many children's books which overshadowed his other work. New poems appeared in an American edition of *Wild Earth* (1916), including the popular "She Moved Through the Fair".

In 1922 the Hawaiian legislature commissioned Colum to write for children the islands' folklore, three volumes resulting from his visit. A book of verse, *Dramatic Legends* (1922), was followed by his first novel, *Castle Conquer* (1923), set in an impoverished nineteenth century, as was *The Flying Swans* (1937). Of the later collections of verse, *Irish Elegies* (1958) is interesting for its portraits of Roger Casement, Griffith, James Joyce (*see page 71*) and others.

The Colums lived in France in the early 1930s, Colum renewing an old friendship with Joyce, for whom he typed parts of *Finnegans Wake*. On returning to America, they both taught comparative literature at Columbia University, becoming US citizens in 1945.When Mary Colum died in 1957, Colum completed their anecdotal *Our Friend James Joyce* (1958). In 1959 he published *Ourselves Alone*, a biography of Griffith begun many years earlier. Colum died in Enfield, Connecticut, on 11 January 1972.

JAMES JOYCE

1882 1941

Joyce was born in Rathgar, Dublin, on 2 February 1882. His father lived beyond his means, and when he lost his post as a rates collector in 1891 the family moved into ever poorer lodgings in north Dublin. Joyce was withdrawn from Clongowes Wood, the fashionable Jesuit College in Co. Kildare, but returned to Jesuit influence at Belvedere College in 1893.He was a prize-winning scholar and had periods of religious fervour, but he also frequented Dublin's prostitutes from the age of fourteen and eventually abandoned Catholicism. He was reading modern languages at University College, Dublin, when the *Fortnightly Review* published his article on "Ibsen's New Drama", which drew praise from the Norwegian dramatist. Joyce thought the Irish Literary Revival backward-looking, but he cultivated W. B. Yeats, George Russell (*see pages 52 & 55*) and others who proved useful to him. He himself had little success as a playwright, and *Exiles*, published in 1918, is seldom performed.

On graduating in 1902 Joyce impractically sought to study medicine at the Sorbonne in Paris, but returned to Dublin because of his mother's terminal illness. He began to write *Stephen Hero*, an unfinished novel which was later reworked as *A Portrait of the Artist as a Young Man*. Russell published in *The Irish Homestead* some stories which later appeared in *Dubliners*.

On 16 June 1904 Joyce went walking at Ringsend, at the Liffey's mouth, with Nora Barnacle, a Galway chambermaid he had met a few days earlier. He chose that date for the events recorded in his novel *Ulysses*, though it was later in the summer that he and Oliver St John Gogarty (*see page 62*) occupied the Martello tower at Sandycove, Co. Dublin, which features in the opening chapter. In October 1904 Joyce and Nora left Dublin. He found work in a language school in Trieste, then part of the Austrian Empire, where his brother Stanislaus joined them in 1905. Not until 1931 were Joyce and Nora married.

In 1907 a collection of poems, *Chamber Music*, was published in London. Joyce returned to Dublin twice in 1909, first to arrange publication of *Dubliners,* then to open a short-lived cinema. On his last visit in 1912, he failed to overcome his publisher's reservations about *Dubliners*, but in 1914 the book was published in London, and the English magazine *The Egoist* began to serialise *A Portrait of the Artist as a Young Man*. During World War I Stanislaus was interned, and Joyce had to move to Zurich in neutral

Switzerland. In 1917 an attack of glaucoma led to the first of many eye operations.

A Portrait was published in America in 1916 and in England in 1917. Joyce's reputation was growing, and in 1918 *The Little Review* in New York began to serialise *Ulysses*. Publication was halted in 1920, and a court subsequently held that the book was pornographic. By then Joyce had settled in Paris, and in 1922 *Ulysses* was published by Sylvia Beach, the American owner of a celebrated Paris bookshop, Shakespeare and Company. She later published a collection of verse, *Pomes Penyeach* (1927). *Ulysses* was finally published in America in 1934, and a British edition followed in 1936. Joyce's final work was *Finnegans Wake* (1939), a compendium of linguistic comedy of almost impenetrable denseness. In 1940 he returned to Zurich, where he died on 13 January 1941.

Ulysses is, of course, Joyce's most important work, and its stream of consciousness technique was widely adopted by other novelists. The book recounts a day in the life of Leopold Bloom, a Jewish advertisement canvasser and cuckold, and his eventual meeting with Stephen Dedalus, hero of *A Portrait*. The chapters correspond roughly with Homer's *Odyssey*, ending with Molly Bloom's famous soliloquy. Just as the book recalls Dublin in fine detail, so it transmutes Joyce's early experiences into memorable fiction. The stories in *Dubliners* are also memorable, notably "The Dead", which John Huston translated into a masterly film in 1987.

The Martello tower is now a Joyce museum. The James Joyce centre at 33 North George Street, Dublin, offers a "*Ulysses* Experience".

ST JOHN ERVINE
1883–1971

Ervine was born in Belfast on 28 December 1883. He left school at fourteen to work in an insurance office and at seventeen moved to London, where he met George Bernard Shaw (*see page 47*) and joined the Fabian Society. In 1911 the Abbey Theatre staged his *Mixed Marriage* in Dublin. It was quickly followed by *The Magnanimous Lover* (1912), *The Critics* (1913), *The Orangeman* (1914) and *John Ferguson* (1915). Ervine was appointed manager of the Abbey in 1915, but the brusque Ulsterman considered it merely one of many repertory theatres and quarrelled with most of its regular players. He soon left to join the army and, as a lieutenant in the Royal Dublin Fusiliers, was wounded in France and had a leg amputated. Returning to London, he became a drama critic, notably for *The Observer*.

Most of the early Abbey plays dealt with self-righteous Ulster Protestant patriarchs shaken by unexpected tribulations. *Jane Clegg*, staged in Manchester in 1913, had an English setting; it later became popular in America, as did *John Ferguson*. During the 1920s, Ervine wrote drawing room comedies for the London stage, notably *Mary Mary Quite Contrary* (1923) and *The First Mrs Fraser* (1929), in which the hero seeks a divorce to remarry his first wife. *Robert's Wife* (1937), with Edith Evans, was in a more serious vein.

Ervine was at his best writing about Ulster, and the Abbey staged notable comedies in *Boyd's Shop* (1936), *William John Mawhinney* (1940) and *Friends and Relations* (1941). His plays were popular in Belfast, where some lesser comedies were premiered. In realistic novels, such as *Mrs Martin's Man* (1914), *The Foolish Lovers* (1920) and *The Wayward Man* (1927), Ervine generally took a more sombre view of Ulster life. He drew substantially on his early life among the small shopkeepers and working class of Belfast's Ballymacarrett district, noting the religious tensions and the narrow provincialism from which his heroes might or might not escape.

He also wrote several biographies. Early studies of Sir Edward Carson (1915) and Charles Stewart Parnell (1925) were followed by more substantial works on General Booth of the Salvation Army (1934), Lord Craigavon (1949), an uncritical assessment reflecting Ervine's strong unionist views, Oscar Wilde (1951) (*see page 45*) and Shaw (1956). In later life he settled in Seaton, Devon, but died in Iping, Sussex, on 24 January 1971.

LENNOX ROBINSON
| 1886–1958

Robinson was born in Douglas, near Cork, on 4 October 1886. His father was a stockbroker who took holy orders in 1892. Poor health meant that Robinson had little formal education, but he was well read and had time to observe life around him. In 1907 he saw an Abbey Theatre company performing in Cork. As he later wrote in *Curtain Up* (1942), W. B. Yeats's *Cathleen ni Houlihan* (*see page 52*) and Lady Gregory's *The Rising of the Moon* (*see page 43*) persuaded him to "sing of what I know". In 1908 the Abbey staged his one-act play *The Clancy Name*, set in west Cork. Rural Cork also featured in *The Cross Roads* (1909) and *Harvest* (1910), and during the next three decades Robinson became the Abbey's most prolific and versatile playwright. Yeats was so impressed that in 1909 he offered Robinson the post of producer and manager, citing Ibsen, who as a young man had been given similar responsibility in Norway.

In a turbulent era Robinson turned to more overtly political themes. In *Patriots* (1912) a revolutionary returns from prison to find his idealism no longer valued. *Dreamers* (1915) deals with Robert Emmet; *The Lost Leader* (1918) is based on the idea that Charles Stewart Parnell might still be alive. However, Robinson scored his greatest success with *The Whiteheaded Boy* (1916), a satirical comedy about a favoured son who disappoints his snobbish family.

Robinson left the Abbey in 1914 and for ten years organised libraries for the Carnegie Trust, but from 1919 he was able to undertake production work again, and in 1923 he joined the Abbey board, helping to restore the theatre's fortunes. The best of his later plays are *The White Blackbird* (1925), *The Big House* (1926), an Ascendancy view of the Troubles, *The Far-Off Hills* (1928), a very popular comedy, and *Drama at Inish* (1934).

Robinson's other writing includes *A Young Man from the South* (1918), an autobiographical novel, *Eight Short Stories* (1919), *Three Homes* (1938), an autobiography written with a brother and sister, and *Ireland's Abbey Theatre* (1951). In 1918 he helped to form the Dublin Drama League, which introduced Irish audiences to modern European and American drama, and in his last years he was a much-travelled adjudicator at amateur drama festivals. He died at Monkstown, Co. Dublin, on 14 October 1958.

FRANCIS LEDWIDGE

1887–1917

Ledwidge, son of a farm labourer, was born on 19 August 1887 outside Slane, Co. Meath. He left school at thirteen and held various jobs, once giving up an apprenticeship in Dublin to walk thirty miles back to the region he loved. He was sacked from a copper mine for organising a strike and was working on the roads when, in 1912, he sent a notebook of poems to the author Lord Dunsany (*see page 61*). Dunsany greeted him as a true poet and introduced his work to influential friends in London and Dublin.

As the Home Rule crisis deepened, Ledwidge became secretary of the Slane corps of the Irish Volunteers. Dunsany had persuaded Herbert Jenkins to publish a collection of his poems under the title *Songs of the Fields*, writing an introduction which recalled Robert Burns and John Clare before dubbing Ledwidge "the poet of the blackbird". However, when war broke out in August 1914, publication was postponed. Ledwidge was now unemployed, and Dunsany settled an allowance on him. When the Slane Volunteers answered John Redmond's call to fight in France, Ledwidge dissented, yet within days joined the Royal Inniskilling Fusiliers. His motives were confused. He was escaping from an unsuccessful romance. He would not have it said he stayed at home while the British army "stood between Ireland and an enemy common to our civilisation". He fought "neither for a principle, nor a people, nor a law, but for the fields along the Boyne, for the birds and the blue sky over them".

Songs of the Fields was published in 1915, shortly before Ledwidge saw service at Gallipoli and Salonika and was hospitalised in Egypt and Manchester. Dunsany now helped Ledwidge collect *Songs of Peace* before the poet was sent to the Western Front. On 31 July 1917 Ledwidge was killed during the third battle of Ypres. *Songs of Peace* was published three months later, and Dunsany made a further compilation, *Last Songs* (1918).

Ledwidge's birthplace, outside Slane on the Drogheda Road, is now a museum. A plaque on the Boyne bridge in Slane draws on his poem on Thomas MacDonagh, executed in 1916: "He shall not hear the bittern cry In the wild sky, where he is lain, Nor voices of the sweeter birds Above the wailing of the rain".

JOYCE CARY

1888–1957

Cary was born in Derry on 7 December 1888. His father, descended from an Anglo-Irish family whose fortunes had declined, was a civil engineer in England. However, the son spent long holidays in the Inishowen peninsula in Co. Donegal, though Castle Cary and other big houses had passed out of the family. At seventeen, with an inherited income of £300, Cary studied art in Edinburgh and Paris before deciding that he could better express himself as a writer.

After reading law at Oxford, Cary set off in 1912 for Montenegro, serving as a Red Cross orderly in two Balkan wars. He had now met his future wife and, when work for Horace Plunkett's co-operative movement in Ireland did not lead to a permanent post, joined the Nigerian political service in 1913. During World War I he served with a Nigerian regiment in the Cameroons campaign until wounded. In 1920 he returned to England, settling in Oxford, where he died on 29 March 1957.

Although he had published some short stories under a pseudonym, Cary struggled for ten years to translate his view of life into a novel. Once *Aissa Saved* (1932) was completed, he wrote with great fluency. It drew on his African years, as did *An American Visitor* (1933), *The African Witch* (1936) and *Mister Johnson* (1939), the last a memorable portrait of a native clerk. Ireland inspired *Castle Corner* (1938) and *A House of Children* (1941), an evocation of summers in Inishowen which won the James Tait Black prize.

Cary next drew on the art world for a complex trilogy, in which each book is narrated by one of three main characters. *Herself Surprised, To Be a Pilgrim* and *The Horse's Mouth* (1941–4) are notable for the anarchic painter Gulley Jimpson. A second, more sombre trilogy dealt with politics: *Prisoner of Grace, Except the Lord* and *Not Honour More* (1952–5). A trilogy on religion was to follow, but Cary was dying; a single, uncompleted novel, *The Captive and the Free*, was published in 1959.

Cary's concern for artistic and political liberty also found an outlet in treatises such as *The Case for African Freedom* (1941) and *Art and Reality* (1956). He returned to Africa in 1943 to script the film *Men of Two Worlds*, and films were also made of *The Horse's Mouth* (1958) and *Mister Johnson* (1990).

HELEN WADDELL

1889–1965

Helen Waddell, youngest child of a Presbyterian missionary from Belfast, was born in Tokyo on 31 May 1889. Her ailing mother returned with her ten children to Belfast and died of typhoid fever in 1892. The daughter went back to Japan after her father married a cousin, but the family were again in Belfast when he died in 1901. Waddell took a first in English at Queen's University, Belfast, but a promising academic career was hindered by the need to nurse her invalid and alcoholic stepmother. Not until the latter died in 1920 was she free to undertake research at Somerville College, Oxford. Nonetheless, in 1913 she had published *Lyrics from the Chinese*, and in 1915 her play *The Spoiled Buddha* was staged in Belfast. Her brother Sam was a successful playwright, notably with *The Drone* (1908), under the name Rutherford Mayne. Although appointed to a lectureship at Oxford, Helen Waddell chose to pursue her literary interests in London and Paris, financing herself through lecturing and a research fellowship. The outcome was *The Wandering Scholars* (1927), which breathed new life into medieval studies. Before the year was out, the book was in its third edition, praised by scholars and treasured by ordinary readers.

Waddell's publishers, Constable, now offered her financial security, and she soon delivered her translations of *Medieval Latin Lyrics* (1929), again a popular success. *Peter Abelard* followed in May 1933 and was in its fifteenth edition by December. The novel deals with the famous love story of Heloise and the philosopher Abelard in twelfth century France; he is deemed a heretic and becomes a monk, while she enters a nunnery. Originally Waddell planned a trilogy, but the other books were never written, despite the urgings of George Russell (*see page 55*), who had also been moved by the letters of Heloise and Abelard and the conflict between physical passion and the spiritual life.

Waddell's other major work is *The Desert Fathers* (1936), a contemplation of eternity, but she continued translation, and *More Latin Lyrics* (1976) was published posthumously. She lectured, reviewed and broadcast, and numbered Max Beerbohm, George Bernard Shaw (*see page 47*) and Stanley Baldwin among her friends. A second play, The *Abbé Prévost*, was staged unsuccessfully in 1935. In her later years, Waddell's intellectual powers failed totally. She died in London on 5 March 1965.

PEADAR O'DONNELL

1893–1986

O'Donnell was born on a small farm near Dungloe, Co. Donegal, on 22 February 1893. He trained as a teacher in Dublin during 1911–13 and was influenced by the revolutionary ideas of James Larkin, James Connolly and Patrick Pearse. Returning to Donegal, he taught in the Innisfree and Aranmore islands, but later moved to Scotland, where he became active in the trade union movement, helping to improve the conditions of "tatiehokers", the migrant Irish potato harvesters.

In 1918 O'Donnell returned to Ireland as an organiser for the Irish Transport and General Workers' Union. During the War of Independence he led a brigade of the Irish Republican Army in Donegal. An opponent of the 1921 Anglo-Irish Treaty, he was in the Four Courts in Dublin when the Civil War broke out, and spent almost two years in prison before escaping from the Curragh. He later edited the republican journal *An Phoblacht*, engaging in a successful campaign against land annuities, but was eventually expelled from the IRA. His socialism also made him unpopular with right-wing Catholic groups.

O'Donnell's first novel, *Storm*, appeared in 1925, but it was *Islanders* (1928) which established his literary reputation. In the novel a woman starves herself so that her children can eat. In *Adrigoole* (1929), based on actual events, a mother and child starve to death while the husband is in prison. O'Donnell's deeply realistic novels centre on the poverty of farming and fishing families in the West of Ireland, and are often didactic in tone. Of his later novels, the best is *The Big Windows* (1955), in which an islandwoman misses the open sky when marriage takes her to a narrow glen. His last book, *Proud Island*, appeared in 1975.

O'Donnell also wrote three autobiographical books: *The Gates Flew Open* (1932), about prison life, *Salud!* (1937), recalling the Spanish Civil War, and *There Will Be Another Day* (1963). In 1940 he and Sean O'Faolain (*see page 83*) founded *The Bell*, which O'Donnell edited from 1946 until its closure in 1954. The magazine provided an important outlet for new Irish writing, as well as taking a liberal stance on matters such as censorship and the 1951 Mother and Child controversy. In later years O'Donnell espoused such causes as nuclear disarmament and agitation against the Vietnam war. He died in Dublin on 13 May 1986.

LIAM O'FLAHERTY

| 1896–1984

O'Flaherty was born on Inishmore, the largest of the Aran islands, on 28 August 1896. In 1908 a visiting priest arranged for him to attend Rockwell College in Co. Tipperary, with a view to taking holy orders, and in 1914 he entered University College, Dublin. A year later, he joined the Irish Guards and in 1917 was wounded and shell-shocked near Arras.

On leaving hospital, O'Flaherty spent three years wandering through Europe and the Americas. He became a communist and in 1922 headed a group of unemployed men who briefly occupied the Rotunda concert rooms in Dublin. When the Civil War broke out, O'Flaherty joined the republicans, but soon left for London.

A short story in the socialist *New Leader* attracted the critic Edward Garnett, who helped O'Flaherty to have his novel of Aran life, *The Neighbour's Wife*, published in 1923. Garnett pointed O'Flaherty to the works of Gogol and particularly Dostoevsky and guided him in writing *The Black Soul* (1924), a largely autobiographical novel. A collection of stories, *Spring Sowing*, also appeared in 1924, and these and later stories of Aran peasants are among his best work. O'Flaherty's first major success was *The Informer* (1925). In portraying the weak and suffering Gypo Nolan, he aimed at "a style based on the technique of the cinema", and John Ford filmed it with great success in 1935.

Other novels followed, notably *Mr Gilhooley* (1926), *The Assassin* (1928) and *Skerrett* (1932), together with *The Life of Tim Healy* (1927), an uncomplimentary biography of the Irish Free State's first governor-general. However, O'Flaherty suffered recurrent depression and bouts of alcoholism, and after his marriage broke down in 1932 he renewed his wanderings. *I Went to Russia* (1931) reflected growing disillusion with communism and *Shame the Devil* (1934) described his problems as a writer.

In *Skerrett*, the story of a melancholic island school master, O'Flaherty deals with the decline of traditional peasant values in the modern world. He treated other substantial Irish themes in *Famine* (1937), set in the 1840s, and *Land* (1946), on the land war of the 1870s. His last novel, *Insurrection* (1950), deals with the 1916 rising. During World War II O'Flaherty lived in the Caribbean, South America and Connecticut, where he wrote the stories in *Two Lovely Beasts* (1948). In 1946 he returned to Dublin, where he died on 7 September 1984.

KATE O'BRIEN

1897–1974

Kate O'Brien was born in Limerick on 3 December 1897. Her mother died when she was five, and she became a boarder in the Laurel Hill convent in Limerick. On graduating from University College, Dublin, she worked on the *Manchester Guardian* and as a governess in Spain. She returned to England to marry a Dutch journalist, but they soon parted. Her play *Distinguished Villa* was well received in 1926, but she preferred the more solitary occupation of novelist.

Her first novel, *Without My Cloak* (1931), won both the Hawthornden and James Tait Black prizes. A chronicle of middle-class Catholic life, it is, in effect, an Irish *Forsyte Saga*. Its theme would be constant throughout her novels, namely the struggle (particularly the struggle of Irishwomen) for individual freedom and love against the constricting demands of family, bourgeois society and Catholic religion.

The heroine of *The Ante-Room* (1934) is torn between love and Catholic conscience, as is *Mary Lavelle* (1936). The latter was banned under the Irish Free State's censorship laws, as was O'Brien's novel of convent life, *The Land of Spices* (1941). Neither Mary's sin nor a brief reference to homosexuality in the later novel could reasonably be called "indecent and obscene", the only grounds for a ban, and O'Brien responded with *Pray for the Wanderer* (1938) and *The Last of Summer* (1943), both critical of the smug puritanism of the Free State under Eamon de Valera.

O'Brien's most successful novel was *That Lady* (1946), set in sixteenth-century Spain. Its heroine is Ana de Mendoza, Princess of Eboli, an independent spirit martyred by the despotic King Philip II. O'Brien adapted it for Broadway, where it enjoyed modest success in 1949 with Katherine Cornell in the title role. A disappointing film version appeared in 1955.

O'Brien returned to Ireland in 1950. She settled in Roundstone, Co. Galway, where she wrote *The Flower of May* (1953). Neither it nor *As Music and Splendour* (1958), set in the world of nineteenth-century Italian opera, was a success. In 1962 she published *My Ireland*, an idiosyncratic pen-portrait not unlike her earlier *Farewell Spain* (1937), for which she was banned from Franco's Spain. She also wrote a biography of the saint *Theresa of Avila* (1951). In 1965 she returned to England and died in Canterbury on 13 August 1974.

C. S. LEWIS

1898–1963

Clive Staples Lewis, Jack to his friends, was born in Belfast on 29 November 1898. A solicitor's son, educated mostly in England, he won a classical scholarship to Oxford University in 1916. Enlisting in the army, he was wounded at Arras in 1918. On resuming his studies, he entered into a curious relationship with a demanding older woman, Janie Moore, following a promise made to her son who was killed in the war. Despite the financial burden, Lewis set up house with Mrs Moore and her daughter, first in Oxford and later at nearby Headington Quarry. In 1932 they were joined by Lewis's elder brother Warnie, who had retired from the army. Lewis remained in the house after Mrs Moore's death in 1951 and in 1956 married an American divorcee, Joy Davidman, to enable her to avoid extradition. This second curious relationship brought unexpected happiness, but his wife died of bone cancer in 1960, and Lewis himself died at home on 22 November 1963.

With a triple first, Lewis became a fellow and tutor of Magdalen College in 1925. An agnostic, he found his views changing, helped by the vigorous weekly discussions of academics known as the Inklings, notably J. R. R. Tolkien. From theism he came to a full acceptance of Christianity - "the most dejected and reluctant convert in England", he later wrote. In 1936 he won the Hawthornden prize with *The Allegory of Love*, but it was *The Screwtape Letters* (1942) which made him internationally famous, together with broadcast talks, later collected as *Mere Christianity* (1952). Screwtape is an elderly devil advising his apprentice nephew, who is having trouble securing the damnation of a young Christian.

Lewis's prominence as a Christian apologist probably hindered his academic career, but following his monumental *English Literature in the Sixteenth Century* (1954), he was appointed to a new Cambridge chair in Medieval and Renaissance English, though he returned regularly to his Oxford home. A science fiction trilogy was followed by the great success of *The Chronicles of Narnia* (1950–56), seven children's books beginning with *The Lion, the Witch and the Wardrobe*. His autobiographical work, *Surprised by Joy* (1955), describing his conversion to Anglo-Catholicism, was also a bestseller. Lewis's marriage to Joy Davidman inspired William Nicholson's play *Shadowlands* (1989), and his unusual life continues to attract biographers and critics.

ELIZABETH BOWEN

1899–1973

Elizabeth Bowen was born in Dublin on 7 June 1899, but her family home was Bowen's Court, a Georgian "big house" in Co. Cork. When she was seven, her barrister father suffered a nervous breakdown and her mother took her to live in Kent. When her mother died in 1912, she was brought up by aunts. The insecurity of these early days left Bowen with a persistent stammer, as well as the sense of transience that pervades her writing.

The first of several collections of short stories, *Encounters*, was published in 1923, the year she married an educationist whose career took them to Oxford. Her first novel, *The Hotel*, was published in 1927. Her second, *The Last September* (1929), recalled the Irish Troubles of the 1920s, the conflicting loyalties of the Anglo-Irish and her brief engagement to a British officer.

Bowen's father died in 1930, and she inherited Bowen's Court, where she entertained generously during holidays. She wrote steadily in the 1930s: *Friends and Relations* (1931), *To the North* (1932), *The House in Paris* (1935). In 1935 she moved to a Regency terrace house overlooking Regent's Park in London. *The Death of the Heart* (1938) is set in just such a house; a story of sexual betrayal, it echoed as always her own life and memories.

The Heat of the Day (1949), dealing with love and espionage, drew on her experiences in war-time London including an affair (not her first) with a Canadian diplomat. It was her first novel for eleven years, though she had published the stories of *The Demon Lover* (1945) as well as a history of *Bowen's Court* and a Dublin memoir, *Seven Winters* (1942). Its success meant Bowen's Court could have its first bathrooms.

Bowen was ill at ease in post-war socialist England. She lectured abroad for the British Council, served on the Royal Commission on Capital Punishment, and wrote a history of the Dublin hotel, *The Shelbourne* (1951). Bowen's Court became her permanent home, but it was a financial burden . Her husband died there in 1952, and the house was demolished after she sold it in 1959. Bowen returned to Oxford, then to Kent, writing *A World of Love* (1955), *The Little Girls* (1964) and *Eva Trout* (1968), the latter winning the James Tait Black prize. She died in London on 22 February 1973.

SEAN O'FAOLAIN

1900–1991

O'Faolain was born John Whelan in Cork on 22 February 1900. His father was a constable in the Royal Irish Constabulary, loyal to the Crown and a pillar of respectability and the son had a frugal childhood, with a Christian Brothers education and much emphasis on prayer and study. O'Faolain later described his family as "shabby-genteel at the lowest possible social level", but holiday visits to an aunt in Co. Limerick introduced him to a freer rural life.

The 1916 rising was a turning point for, although O'Faolain initially shared his father's hostility to the rebels, the subsequent executions awakened quite different feelings. He became a fluent Irish speaker, adopting the Irish version of his name. After entering University College, Cork, in 1918 he joined the Irish Volunteers, out of which the Irish Republican Army emerged.

O'Faolain saw little action during the War of Independence, but during the Civil War he made IRA bombs and spent some months hiding in the mountains. Later he became director of publicity for the whole republican movement, but already he was becoming disillusioned with republicanism, which seemed to have no coherent social or economic policies. British rule, he could see, was being replaced by a bourgeois society in which the Roman Catholic Church would exercise great influence.

He eventually returned to university in Cork, and in 1926 won a Commonwealth Fellowship to Harvard University, where his interest in creative writing developed. In 1928 he married Eileen Gould, whom he had met when learning Irish in west Cork, and they determined to return to Ireland; as Eileen O'Faolain she later wrote popular children's stories. Initially, O'Faolain took a teaching job in Middlesex but, with the success of his first collection of short stories, *Midsummer Night Madness* (1932), and a subsidy from his publishers, he was able to return to Ireland in 1933.

If O'Faolain hoped for revolutionary change following the election of a Fianna Fáil government in 1932, he was soon disappointed. His first book was banned in the Irish Free State, and in the following years he was to conduct a vigorous campaign against censorship, notably in *The Bell*, the periodical he founded in 1940. His first novel, *A Nest of Simple Folk* (1934), draws on his own life, its young hero becoming alienated from his parents as he adopts the ideals of earlier generations of Irish nationalists. *Bird Alone* (1936) and *Come Back to Erin* (1940) treat similar dilemmas, but none of his heroes find ultimate success or satisfaction; the new bourgeois Ireland offers them little comfort.

O'Faolain also published biographies of Eamon de Valera (1933 & 1939), Constance Markievicz (1934), Wolfe Tone (1937), Daniel O'Connell (1938), Hugh O'Neill, Earl of Tyrone (1942) and Cardinal Newman (1952). The most substantial is the O'Connell biography, *King of the Beggars*, in which, as elsewhere, he tends to project on to his subject his own ambivalent feelings about Ireland. The early study of de Valera is hagiography; by 1939 O'Faolain found the Irish leader provincial and isolationist, and in a portrait of *The Irish* (1937) he criticised corruption and false patriotism in the Irish middle classes.

It is in the short story that O'Faolain is most accomplished, and he has been called the Irish Chekhov. *Midsummer Night Madness* contains notable accounts of Ireland in a state of war, and it was followed by collections such as *A Purse of Coppers* (1937), *The Man Who Invented Sin* (1948) and *I Remember! I Remember!* (1961). The stories in *Foreign Affairs* (1976) reflect both his own cosmopolitanism and a more outward-looking Ireland.

After O'Faolain gave up editorship of *The Bell* in 1946, his stories became more divorced from any political or social context. He lived in Italy for ten years, writing the travel books *A Summer in Italy* (1949) and *South to Sicily* (1953). His autobiography *Vive Moi!* appeared in 1964, and works of criticism included *The Short Story* (1948) and a fine study of modern novelists, *The Vanishing Hero* (1956). He died in Dun Laoghaire, Co. Dublin, on 21 April 1991.

PAUL VINCENT CARROLL

1900–1968

Carroll was born at Blackrock, Co. Louth, on 10 July 1900. While training as a teacher in Dublin, he developed an interest in drama, seeing in the Abbey Theatre "the spiritual rebirth of the Irish race". Resenting clerical control of Irish education, he became a teacher in Glasgow in 1921 and began submitting plays to the Abbey.

In 1930 *The Watched Pot* was staged at the experimental Peacock Theatre; it is a sombre drama, owing something to J. M. Synge (*see page 56*), about a family hoping to collect a dying man's insurance. After *Things That Are Caesar's* (1932) was staged in Dublin, the Abbey took the play to America, and in 1933 it was a London success. In the play, a materialistic mother forces marriage on her daughter with a priest's help. Ibsen was an influence on Carroll's work, and in a later revision the daughter (like Nora in *The Doll's House*) liberates herself from a dull existence.

In 1937 the success of *Shadow and Substance*, which won a prize from the New York drama critics, enabled Carroll to give up teaching. The play features two proud men, Canon Skerritt and the schoolmaster O'Flingsley, whose conflict is mediated by the gentle young house keeper Brigid. O'Carroll's anti-clericalism is again evident, and O'Flingsley voices the author's contempt for Irish education.

The White Steed (1939) also has a strong anti-clerical element, and the Abbey rejected it. However, it also won a critics' prize in New York. In the play, a young school master is persuaded to rebel against a fanatical priest; the title draws on the legend of Oisín, who was carried off to the land of eternal youth. W. B. Yeats (*see page 52*) also used the legend, and Carroll had the same feeling for an heroic Irish past.

Carroll's later plays, too full of symbolism, were less successful. They include *Kindred* (1939), *The Old Foolishness* (1940) and *The Wise Have Spoken* (1944), as well as plays with a Scottish setting and several for children. He was a founder of the Glasgow Citizens' Theatre in 1943, but moved to England in 1945, writing for cinema and television. His later satires, *The Devil Came From Dublin* (1951) and *The Wayward Saint* (1955), show a return to his earlier astringency and command of dialogue. Carroll died in Bromley, Kent, on 20 October 1968.

DENIS JOHNSTON

1901–1984

Johnston was born in Dublin on 18 June 1901. His father an Ulster Presbyterian nationalist, later became a Supreme Court judge in the Irish Free State. Johnston was educated at Cambridge University, where he was president of the union, and Harvard, and practised as a barrister for ten years before joining the BBC in 1936.

Johnston's early work with the Dublin Drama League was noted by W. B. Yeats (*see page 52*), who in 1928 invited him to direct *King Lear* at the Abbey. The Abbey had already rejected Johnston's expressionist satire *Shadowdance*, but it was accepted by the new Gate Theatre under the title *The Old Lady Says "No!"*. The words, an apparent reference to Lady Gregory (*see page 43*), had been attached to the rejected manuscript. The play was staged in 1929, with Micheál Mac Liammóir as the Irish rebel Robert Emmet, a dream sequence dramatising his disillusion with modern Ireland.

A more conventional play, *The Moon in the Yellow River* (1931), was accepted by the Abbey and was a hit in London and New York. It drew on issues raised by the controversial Shannon hydro-electricity scheme, bringing industrialisation to a peasant society, and on conflicts unresolved by the Civil War. *A Bride for the Unicorn* (1933), *Storm Song* (1934), inspired by the filming of *Man of Aran*, *Blind Man's Buff* (1936), a court-room drama, and *The Golden Cuckoo* (1939) were less successful.

As a BBC war correspondent, Johnston flew with bombers, recorded Yugoslav partisans singing "Tipperary" and reported on the Buchenwald concentration camp. *Nine Rivers from Jordan* (1953) is an unusual spiritual odyssey covering his war years. *The Brazen Horn* (1968) is also autobiographical. Johnston was briefly director of programmes in BBC television, but from 1950 held a number of academic posts in America. He returned to Ireland in 1973, became the Abbey's first play editor and died in Dublin on 8 August 1984.

Of his later plays, *The Dreaming Dust* (1940) reflected deep research into the life of Jonathan Swift (*see page 6*), later published as *In Search of Swift* (1959). *Strange Occurrence on Ireland's Eye* (1956) was another court-room drama, and *The Scythe and the Sunset* (1955) drew on his recollections of the 1916 rising, presenting a more intellectual view than Seán O'Casey's *The Plough and the Stars* (*see page 67*), whose title he parodied.

FRANK O'CONNOR

1903–1966

O'Connor was born in Cork on 17 September 1903. His real name was Michael Francis O'Donovan, and his pen name came from his own middle name and his mother's maiden name. As his autobiographical *An Only Child* (1961) makes clear, he was much more attached to his mother than to his father, a labourer and former army bandsman too prone to drunken rages. O'Connor had an impoverished childhood and suffered poor health, but at school was fortunate to be taught by Daniel Corkery (*see page 60*), who encouraged an interest in literature and the Irish language.

O'Connor left school at fourteen and worked as a railway clerk. He joined the Irish Volunteers in 1919, but saw little action in the War of Independence. During the Civil War he took the republican side and in 1923 was captured and interned at Gormanstown, Co. Meath. He made himself unpopular with fellow prisoners by refusing to join in a hunger strike, and emerged disillusioned with republicanism's lack of humanity and its worship of martyrdom.

On his release, O'Connor became an assistant librarian in Sligo and then in Wicklow. George Russell (*see page 55*) invited him to contribute to *The Irish Statesman*, and he adopted his pen-name for his short stories and poems. He returned to Cork for three years, founding a drama society there, but in 1928 abandoned its narrow provincialism to take up a library post in Dublin.

O'Connor quickly entered Dublin's literary circles and became a director of the Abbey Theatre, but resigned after the death of W.B. Yeats (*see page 52*) in 1939. In *My Father's Son* (1969), O'Connor opined that "mediocrity was in control and against mediocrity there is no challenge or appeal". The Abbey had staged his *In the Train* (1937), *The Invincibles* (1938), a collaboration with Hugh Hunt, and *Moses' Rock* (1938).

O'Connor's first collection of short stories, *Guests of the Nation* (1931), drew on his experiences in the Troubles a decade or so earlier. The stories contrast the idealism of the combatants with the cruel realities of the struggle. In the title story, two British soldiers are held hostage, become friendly with their captors, then are shot in a reprisal killing. Significantly, O'Connor found a subject for biography in Michael Collins, *The Big Fellow* (1937), who had fought on the other side in the Civil War. He resigned his library post in 1938, accepting the advice of publisher Harold Macmillan that he must decide whether to be a good writer or a good public servant.

O 'Connor wrote two novels *The Saint and Mary Kate* (1932) and *Dutch Interior* (1940), but his international reputation rested on the short stories collected under such titles as *Bones of Contention* (1935), *Crab Apple Jelly* (1944) and *Domestic Relations* (1957). His exploration of the sexual repressions of Irish life brought him into conflict with the Irish censors, and some of his books were banned in Ireland. In the 1940s he became poetry editor of *The Bell*, edited by his friend Sean O'Faolain (*see page 83*), and the magazine campaigned against censorship. O'Connor was also active in campaigning for the preservation of Ireland's archaeological and historical remains, and *Irish Miles* (1947) describes his bicycle trips in search of the vanishing past.

As a poet, O'Connor is now best known for his translations from Irish, collected in volumes such as *The Wild Bird's Nest* (1932), *The Fountain of Magic* (1939) and *Kings, Lords and Commons* (1959). The last was banned in Ireland, as was his translation of *The Midnight Court* (1945), Brian Merriman's bawdy eighteenth century account of a fairy trial.

In later years, he held a number of academic posts in America, publishing critical works derived from his lectures. The most notable are *The Mirror in the Roadway* (1956), on nineteenth-century novelists, and *The Lonely Voice* (1963), a study of the short story, which he believed has "at its most characteristic something we do not often find in the novel – an intense awareness of human loneliness". O'Connor returned to Ireland in 1960 and died in Dublin on 10 March 1966.

PATRICK KAVANAGH

1904 1967

Kavanagh was born near Inniskeen, Co. Monaghan, on 21 October 1904. His father was a village cobbler who farmed a few acres, and Kavanagh was apprenticed to the same trade. After a weekly newspaper published some of his poems in 1928, he contributed to *The Irish Statesman*; on visiting its editor, George Russell, *(see page 55)* in 1930, he returned with an armful of books from Russell's library. Reading Liam O'Flaherty and Frank O'Connor *(see pages 79 & 87)* alongside Dostoevsky and Whitman persuaded Kavanagh that an Irishman of humble origins could succeed as a writer.

His first book, *Ploughman and Other Poems*, was published in 1936, followed by *The Green Fool* (1938), a semi-fictional autobiography which led to a libel action. Oliver St John Gogarty *(see page 62)* was awarded £100 for a passage in which Kavanagh recalled an uninvited visit: "I mistook Gogarty's white-robed maid for his wife – or his mistress. I expected every poet to have a spare mistress".

Kavanagh moved to Dublin in 1939, finding journalistic work and becoming a familiar but abrasive figure in literary circles. In 1942 *The Great Hunger*, a long poem about the squalor of rural life, confirmed his reputation. It describes the life of Patrick Maguire, a small farmer worn down and ultimately defeated by the paralysing demands of poor land, oppressive Church and ageing mother. Kavanagh's novel *Tarry Flynn* (1948) takes a more romantic view, its hero escaping to find fortune elsewhere, but still expresses the pain Kavanagh felt at leaving "Shancoduff's watery hills" and other loved places.

Later collections of verse included *A Soul for Sale* (1947), *Come Dance with Kitty Stobling* (1960) and *Collected Poems* (1964). In "malignant Dublin", Kavanagh's verse became more comic and satiric, and he was jealous of writers who achieved the popular and financial success which always eluded him. However, he wrote lyrically of the district around Baggot Street Bridge and the Grand Canal, where he lived. His most important journalistic venture was the short-lived *Kavanagh's Weekly*, which he and his supportive brother Peter launched in 1952 as a literary and political journal. In 1954 he lost a libel action against a Dublin weekly, *The Leader*, which had published a critical profile. Kavanagh died in Dublin on 30 November 1967.

Inniskeen has many Kavanagh reminders, including a small museum.

SAMUEL BECKETT

| 1906–1989

Beckett, the son of a quantity surveyor of Huguenot descent, was born in Dublin. The author always insisted he was born on Good Friday, 13 April 1906, but 13 May is on his birth certificate. He was educated at Portora Royal School in Enniskillen, Co. Fermanagh, and at Trinity College, Dublin, where he studied French and Italian with distinction. A sportsman, Beckett became the first Nobel Prize winner to appear in cricket's *Wisden*.

He taught for some months at Campbell College in Belfast – "the cream of Ulster" said a colleague, to which Beckett replied, "Yes, rich and thick" – before taking up an exchange lectureship in Paris, where he met James Joyce (*see page 71*). Beckett helped Joyce with his work and often read to the poorly sighted author. His own academic reputation was secured by a critical study of Marcel Proust (1931).

Beckett returned to TCD in 1930 to lecture in French, but soon resigned. During the next few years he travelled widely in Europe, lived for a time in Chelsea, and supplemented a modest annuity with literary translations. Beckett's three great influences were Joyce, Ireland and illness. When he visited his family in Dublin, the city's oppressive Catholic atmosphere would induce physical illness, and like Joyce he had to leave. In 1939 he was in Dublin, but preferred "France at war to Ireland at peace".

Beckett had settled in the Montparnasse quarter of Paris in 1937 and in 1938 published his comic novel *Murphy*. In the same year he was stabbed in a street incident and was helped to hospital by a young woman, Suzanne Deschevaux-Dumesnil; they lived together for many years, finally marrying in 1961. Both served in the French Resistance during World War II, Beckett escaping arrest to work as a farm labourer in unoccupied France.

Beckett returned to Paris in 1947 and thereafter largely wrote in French, later translating his work into English. In little over two years he wrote the works which are the foundation of his reputation: the novels *Molloy* (1951), *Malone Dies* (1951) and *The Unnamable* (1953), and above all the play *Waiting for Godot.*

Beckett has been described as the greatest experimenter in fiction since Joyce, a playwright more radical in innovation than Pirandello, a writer of imaginative power comparable to Kafka. *Godot* received its first stage production in Paris in 1953, and its success brought Beckett international fame, though he remained so reclusive that he refused to attend the Nobel

Prize ceremony in 1969. In his tragi-comedy, the two tramps Vladimir and Estragon await "with a large measure of despair and a small measure of hope" the promised arrival – of what? "If I knew who Godot was," Beckett noted, "I would have said so in the play."

None of Beckett's later plays had quite the same success, but they presented some memorable theatrical images: Nell in *Endgame* (1956) announcing from a dustbin that "Nothing is funnier than unhappiness"; Winnie in *Happy Days* (1966), up to her waist and later her neck in sand; the hero of *Krapp's Last Tape* (1958) reliving his life with a tape-recorder. The Irish actors Jack MacGowran and Patrick Magee were among a small number of interpreters who enjoyed Beckett's confidence, and indeed the plays have an elusive Irish quality in their words and rhythms of speech. Beckett's success paved the way for other practitioners of the theatre of the absurd, such as Ionesco and Pinter; like them, he found himself writing shorter and shorter plays which lacked the earlier comic invention.

One anecdote has Beckett emerging from a restaurant into sunshine, with his companion saying, "On a day like this, isn't it good to be alive?" To which the reply was, "I wouldn't go quite so far as that." By the time Beckett died in Paris on 22 December 1989, he had spawned an academic growth industry comparable to that surrounding Joyce, but only *Godot* has won a popular audience, and for its comedy rather than its fundamentally pessimistic message.

LOUIS MacNEICE

1907–1963

MacNeice, as he wrote, was "born in Belfast between the mountains and the gantries To the hooting of lost sirens and the clang of trams" on 12 September 1907. His father was rector of Carrickfergus, Co. Antrim, from 1908 to 1931, and eventually bishop of Down, Connor and Dromore. MacNeice was educated in England, and at Oxford University associated with poets such as W. H. Auden and Stephen Spender.

His first book of verse, *Blind Fireworks*, was published in 1930, when he became a classics lecturer in Birmingham, and his reputation grew steadily. However, his only novel, *Roundabout Way* (1932), was a failure, and he had little success writing for the stage. A second collection of astringently witty *Poems* appeared in 1935, and after he moved to Bedford College in London, a journey with Auden led to their *Letters from Iceland* (1937). He had earlier visited Spain with the future traitor Anthony Blunt, a lifelong friend from schooldays, and returned there in 1939.

MacNeice was left-wing, but, unlike Blunt, never a communist. A summation of his life and intellectual outlook appeared in *Autumn Journal* (1939), possibly his finest work. The long poem takes in his Irish childhood, his English education, the roots of the Munich crisis and the threatening future foreshadowed by Franco's victory in the Spanish Civil War.

MacNeice left for America in 1940; Auden and Christopher Isherwood had already been criticised for deserting Britain, and he soon returned through fear of "having missed so much history, lost touch". He joined the BBC in 1941, finding new creative possibilities in radio. His play *The Dark Tower* (1946) is recognised as a classic of the medium; a notable version of *Faust* (1961) marked Goethe's bicentenary. MacNeice left the BBC in 1961, after his second marriage failed, but was working on an underground recording when he caught a chill. He died of pneumonia in London on 3 September 1963.

MacNeice was a prolific writer, and volumes of poetry appeared regularly. In 1941 he published a critical volume on *The Poetry of W. B. Yeats* (*see page 52*) and increasingly (like Yeats) looked to Irish landscape and mythology as a source of inspiration and identity. *Autumn Sequel* (1954) complemented his 1939 poem, its sombre mood reflecting the passing years, but MacNeice's post-war poetry is generally less effective than his earlier work.

FLANN O'BRIEN

| 1911–1966

Flann O'Brien is the pen-name of Brian O'Nolan (or O Nualláin), known also to readers of *The Irish Times* as Myles na Gopaleen (or gCopaleen). He was born into an Irish-speaking family in Strabane, Co. Tyrone, on 5 October 1911, and was the son of an excise officer who prospered in Dublin following the establishment of the Irish Free State.

O'Nolan studied at University College, Dublin, where his comic talents became apparent in a student publication, *Comhthrom Féinne*, and in 1934 he helped to set up a short-lived humorous magazine, *Blather*. Billiards, poker and alcohol also figured strongly in his life. In 1935 he joined the Irish civil service.

When O'Nolan submitted his comic novel *At Swim Two-Birds* to Longmans, the author Graham Greene praised it as being in the line of *Tristram Shandy* and James Joyce's *Ulysses* (*see page 71*). "We have had books inside books before but O'Nolan takes Pirandello and Gide a long way further", Greene wrote. "The screw is turned until you have (a) a book about a man called Trellis who is (b) writing a book about certain characters who (c) are turning the tables on Trellis by writing about him".

The book was published in 1939 under the pen-name Flann O'Brien, which O'Nolan had previously used in letters in *The Irish Times* criticising Sean O'Faolain and Frank O'Connor (*see pages 83 & 87*). It sold poorly and much of the first edition was destroyed in 1940 during an air raid on London.

Further correspondence in *The Irish Times* led to an invitation to contribute a regular column, and the first "Cruiskeen Lawn" (little brimming jug) appeared in 1940. The pen-name Myles na Gopaleen (Myles of the little horses) was drawn from Gerald Griffin's *The Collegians* (*see page 28*). The mythical Myles lived in Santry, on the edge of the city, and regular appearances were made by the Brother, the bibulous Keats and Chapman, whose stories ended in tortuous puns, and the Plain People of Ireland. Myles's Research Bureau invented emergency trousers with long pockets for storing bottles of stout while his Escort Service provided ventriloquists so that the ignorant could appear to make intelligent remarks at parties. If *At Swim Two Birds* owed an unacknowledged debt to Joyce, whom he called "that refurbisher of skivvies' stories", Cruiskeen Lawn had a flavour of Beachcomber in the *Daily Express*.

O'Nolan was cynical about attempts to restore the Irish language, and in 1941 parodied an autobiography he admired, Tomás Ó Criomhthain's *An t-Oileánach* (The Islandman). *An Béal Bocht* appeared under Myles's authorship and was translated as *The Poor Mouth* in 1973. In a letter to Seán O'Casey (*see page 67*) O'Nolan described Irish as an unknown quantity enabling writers to transform the English language even if, like Joyce, they had little knowledge of it.

In 1940, Longmans had rejected Flann O'Brien's second novel, *The Third Policeman*. A nightmarishly comic vision of hell, the book is notable for a theory that the exchange of atoms between men and bicycles on rocky roads means that many people are half bicycles. The author considered turning it into a play, but instead Myles wrote *Faustus Kelly* (1943) for the Abbey Theatre. Kelly sells his soul to the devil for a seat in the Irish parliament, and the play reflected O'Nolan's low opinion of politicians. His adaptation of *The Insect Play* (1943) by Karel and Josef Capek played briefly at the Gate Theatre.

In 1953 O'Nolan retired from the civil service on grounds of ill health, a consequence of his heavy drinking. His departure was hastened by sour and irascible Cruiskeen Lawn columns which overstepped the bounds permitted to civil servants. He supplemented a modest pension with freelance journalism.

At Swim-Two-Birds had long been cherished by a coterie of admirers, and in 1960 it was republished to acclaim. Despite his drinking, Flann O'Brien settled down to write *The Hard Life* (1961), a bleak comedy set in Joyce's Dublin, and *The Dalkey Archive* (1964). O'Nolan died in Dublin on 1 April 1966. *The Third Policeman* was published in 1967.

WALTER MACKEN

1915–1967

Macken was born in Galway on 3 May 1915. At seventeen he joined the Taibhdhearc na Gaillimhe, the city's Irish language theatre, soon becoming its leading producer and actor. One of the plays he wrote in Irish told the story of the Claddagh fishermen in Galway, and Macken reworked his material for the novel *Rain on the Wind* (1950).

When Macken turned to writing in English, *Mungo's Mansion* was staged by the Abbey Theatre in Dublin in 1946. He moved to Dublin, enjoying great success with *Home Is the Hero* (1952), its central figure a violent dullard returning from prison and attempting to reassert his authority over his family. *Twilight of a Warrior* (1955) also deals with a similarly alienated protagonist, in this case a republican hero who in peacetime can only find victory in bullying the members of his family.

Macken was a well-regarded actor in Dublin and had a New York success in 1948 in Michael J. Molloy's *The King of Friday's Men*. He starred in the 1959 film version of *Home Is the Hero* and in the 1962 film of Brendan Behan's *The Quare Fellow* (*see page 98*).

His first novel, *Quench the Moon* (1948), was quickly followed by *I Am Alone* (1949); both were banned by the Irish censors, as was *The Bogman* (1952). The success of *Rain on the Wind* encouraged Macken to move to Oughterard, Co. Galway, where he embarked on his best known work, the trilogy of historical novels portraying ordinary people caught up in tumultuous events. *Seek the Fair Land* (1959) is set in Cromwellian Ireland, *The Silent People* (1962) in the famine years of the nineteenth century, and *The Scorching Wind* (1964) in the period from the 1916 rising to the troubled birth of the Irish Free State.

Macken also wrote short stories, set in the West of Ireland and collected under such titles as *The Green Hills* (1956) and *God Made Sunday* (1962). *Island of the Great Yellow Ox* (1966) and *Flight of the Doves* (1968), filmed in 1971, were written for children. In 1966 Macken returned briefly to the Abbey as artistic director, before settling at Menlo, outside Galway city. He had just completed his novel *Brown Lord of the Mountain* (1967) when he died suddenly on 22 April 1967.

BRIAN MOORE

| 1921–1999

Moore was born in Belfast on 25 August 1921. His elderly father, a surgeon at the Roman Catholic Mater Hospital, had been a friend of the Irish revolutionary Roger Casement, and one of Moore's uncles was Eoin MacNeill, who had been chief of staff of the Irish Volunteers and later a government minister in the Irish Free State.

Educated at St. Malachy's College, Moore decided against a medical career. Instead, with the outbreak of World War II, he took a job in air raid precautions, and later recalled the German bombing of Belfast in *The Emperor of Ice-Cream* (1965). In 1943 he left Belfast to work for the Ministry of War Transport. After the war he worked in Poland for the United Nations Relief and Rehabilitation Administration. He had by now abandoned Roman Catholicism.

In 1948 Moore emigrated to Canada, working for the Montreal Gazette as proof-reader and reporter, an experience reflected in *The Luck of Ginger Coffey* (1960). His first books were thrillers, written under the pen-name Michael Bryan. He set his first novel as Brian Moore in the claustrophobic world of Belfast's Catholic minority. It was published in London after several American publishers had rejected it.

Judith Hearne (1955), an alcoholic spinster living in a boarding-house, suffers a breakdown when her romantic fantasies about an Ulsterman home from America come to nothing. In 1956 the novel was published in America as *The Lonely Passion of Judith Hearne*. When it was filmed under this title in 1987, the setting was unwisely changed to Dublin.

Moore's second Belfast novel was *The Feast of Lupercal* (1957), whose central figure is a repressed schoolmaster as lonely as Judith Hearne. It offers an unflattering account of a Catholic school, with a strict regime of corporal punishment and learning by rote.

In *An Answer from Limbo* (1962) an Irish widow comes to New York to live with her son and American wife. It is one of several novels in which the traditional values of Catholic Ireland conflict with the more liberal mores of the New World. Moore had moved to New York in 1960, and the novel's portrait of an uneasy marriage possibly echoed Moore's own divorce. He moved to California, where he wrote the screenplay for *Torn Curtain* (1966), one of Alfred Hitchcock's worst films. By now a Canadian citizen,

Moore returned regularly to Nova Scotia, but he made his home in Malibu, marrying for a second time.

With *I Am Mary Dunne* (1968), narrated by a much married Canadian facing an identity crisis in New York, Moore again demonstrated his skill in writing about women. It would be equally evident in *The Doctor's Wife* (1976), in which a frustrated Belfast housewife embarks on an affair with a young American in Paris, and in *The Temptation of Eileen Hughes* (1981), in which an innocent shopgirl infatuates her employer.

There is a great variety to Moore's work. In *Fergus* (1970), an expatriate Irish scriptwriter is confronted, in a series of surreal hallucinations, by figures from his past. *Catholics* (1972), a novella which was also filmed, examined the effects of doctrinal changes on an isolated monastic community on an Irish island.

In *The Great Victorian Collection* (1975), a Canadian academic dreams of a collection of Victorian artefacts and finds they have magically materialised outside his motel in California. In *The Mangan Inheritance* (1979) an unsuccessful New York writer goes to Ireland to find if he is descended from the poet James Clarence Mangan (*see page 27*). In *Cold Heaven* (1983), a lapsed Catholic conceals the fact that she has seen a vision of the Virgin Mary.

Cold Heaven, in which a husband's body disappears after he has been pronounced dead, has elements of a thriller, and some of Moore's later books belong to that genre. In *The Colour of Blood* (1987), set behind the Iron Curtain, a Catholic cardinal's life is threatened by growing civil unrest. *Lies of Silence* (1990) deals with moral issues posed by a bombing incident in Belfast. *The Statement* (1995) describes the pursuit of a war criminal.

Moore further demonstrated his versatility with novels such as *Black Robe* (1985) a gory account of a canoe journey undertaken by an early Jesuit missionary in Quebec; *No Other Life* (1993), on the political rise of a black priest in the Caribbean; and *The Magician's Wife* (1997), dealing with the conflict between Christianity and the Muslim world. He may have abandoned religion in his early years, but his work never does. Moore died in Malibu on 11 January 1999.

BRENDAN BEHAN

1923–1964

Behan was born in Dublin on 9 February 1923. His father was a house painter who had been imprisoned as a republican towards the end of the Civil War, and from an early age Behan was steeped in Irish history and patriotic ballads; however, there was also a strong literary and cultural atmosphere in his home.

At fourteen Behan was apprenticed to his father's trade. He was already a member of Fianna Éireann, the youth organisation of the Irish Republican Army, and a contributor to *The United Irishman*. When the IRA launched a bombing campaign in England in 1939, Behan was trained in explosives, but was arrested the day he landed in Liverpool. In February 1940 he was sentenced to three years' Borstal detention. He spent two years in a Borstal in Suffolk, making good use of its excellent library.

In 1942, back in Dublin, Behan fired at a detective during an IRA parade and was sentenced to fourteen years' penal servitude. Again he broadened his education, becoming a fluent Irish speaker. During his first months in Mountjoy prison, Sean O'Faolain (*see page 83*) published Behan's description of his Borstal experiences in *The Bell*.

Behan was released in 1946 as part of a general amnesty and returned to painting. He would serve other prison terms, either for republican activity or as a result of his drinking, but none of such length. For some years Behan concentrated on writing verse in Irish. He lived in Paris for a time before returning in 1950 to Dublin, where he cultivated his reputation as one of the more rambunctious figures in the city's literary circles.

In 1954 Behan's play *The Quare Fellow* was well received in the tiny Pike Theatre. However, it was the 1956 production at Joan Littlewood's Theatre Royal in Stratford, East London, that brought Behan a wider reputation – significantly assisted by a drunken interview on BBC television. Thereafter, Behan was never free from media attention, and he in turn was usually ready to play the drunken Irishman.

The "quare fellow", never seen on stage, is a condemned man in prison. His imminent execution touches the lives of the other prisoners, the warders and the hangman, and the play is in part a protest against capital punishment. More important, though, its blend of tragedy and comedy underlines the survival of the prisoners' humanity in their inhumane environment. How much the broader London version owed to Joan Littlewood is a matter of debate. Comparing him with another alcoholic writer, Dylan Thomas, a friend said that "Dylan wrote *Under Milkwood* and Brendan wrote under Littlewood".

Behan's second play, *An Giall* (1958), was commissioned by Gael Linn, the Irish-language organisation. Behan translated the play into English and it was Joan Littlewood's production of *The Hostage* (1958) which led to success in London and New York. As before Behan's tragi-comedy deals with a closed world, in this case a Dublin brothel where the IRA imprison an English soldier, but Littlewood diluted the naturalism of the Irish version with interludes of music-hall singing and dancing. Behan's autobiographical *Borstal Boy* also appeared in 1958, and its early chapters on prison life are among his best work. By then, however, he was a victim of his own celebrity, and alcoholism and diabetes were taking their toll. His English publishers suggested that, instead of the writing he now found difficult, he dictate to a tape recorder. The first outcome was *Brendan Behan's Island* (1962), a readable collection of anecdotes and opinions in which it was apparent that Behan had moved away from the republican extremism of his youth.

Tape-recording also produced *Brendan Behan's New York* (1964) and *Confessions of an Irish Rebel* (1965), a disappointing sequel to *Borstal Boy*. A collection of newspaper columns from the 1950s, published as *Hold Your Hour and Have Another* (1963), merely underlined the inferiority of his later work. When Behan died in Dublin on 20 March 1964, an IRA guard of honour escorted his coffin. One newspaper described it as the biggest funeral since those of Michael Collins and Charles Stewart Parnell.

J. P. DONLEAVY

1926–

James Patrick Donleavy was born in Brooklyn, New York, on 23 April 1926. His parents had both come from Ireland. During World War II, Donleavy served in the US Navy, and thus earned the right to a free university education. In 1946 he entered Trinity College, Dublin.

Among his fellow Americans at college was Gainor Crist, a law student and serious drinker, who was to become the model for Sebastian Dangerfield, the anti-hero of Donleavy's first and most famous comic novel, *The Ginger Man*. The two Americans soon became part of the Dublin literary scene, in which art and alcohol are never far apart.

Donleavy was also a talented painter, and was exhibiting his work long before he found a publisher, the unconventional Olympia Press in Paris, for his novel in 1955. *The Ginger Man* appeared around the time that English writers such as John Osborne and Arnold Wesker were being labelled "angry young men". Donleavy's Dangerfield, wayward and irresponsible, struck a chord with a critical young generation much as Osborne's Jimmy Porter would do in *Look Back in Anger*.

In conservative Ireland, Donleavy's work inevitably had its critics. A stage version of *The Ginger Man* was halted in Dublin in 1959, through the intervention of the Roman Catholic archbishop of Dublin. It was soon staged in London and New York, and a later Irish production passed without incident.

Donleavy is a prolific writer, though none of his later serio-comic novels has matched the fame of *The Ginger Man*. Some critics find them too much a repetition of that first mixture of broad comedy, sexual fantasy and underlying despair. They include *A Singular Man* (1964), *The Beastly Beatitudes of Balthazar B.* (1968), *A Fairy Tale of New York* (1973), *The Destinies of Darcy Dancer, Gentleman* (1977) and *That Darcy, That Dancer, That Gentleman* (1990).

A number of the novels have been adapted for the stage, but none has achieved major success. Many of his books are set in America, but he has written perceptively of his chosen home in *Ireland: In All Her Sins and in Some of Her Graces* (1986) and *A Singular Country* (1989).

Donleavy has been twice married and twice divorced. He has largely lived in Ireland, and in 1967 became an Irish citizen. Since 1969, writers have enjoyed tax exemption, and Donleavy has been able to enjoy the life of a country squire in a succession of handsome houses.

WILLIAM TREVOR

| 1928–

Trevor was born in Mitchelstown, Co. Cork, on 30 August 1928. His full name was William Trevor Cox, and he was the son of a bank official, whose occupation meant that the family frequently moved from one provincial town to another. He attended many schools and, although a Protestant, was occasionally tutored by a nun or a Christian Brother. It was an experience which would later allow him, perhaps uniquely among Irish writers, to describe events equally well from a Protestant or Catholic perspective.

His last school was St. Columba's College in Dublin, where art was taught by the sculptor Oisín Kelly. Trevor's early ambition was to become a sculptor, and he continued wood carving while taking a history degree at Trinity College, Dublin. On graduating in 1950, he became a schoolmaster. He taught first in Co. Armagh, then moved to England in 1953. He taught art in Rugby, then moved to Somerset, where he enjoyed a modest reputation as a sculptor of religious works.

He also began to write, and his first novel, *A Standard of Behaviour*, was published in 1958. With a family to support, Trevor took a job in advertising in London in 1960. When his second novel, *The Old Boys* (1964), won the Hawthornden Prize, he opted for full-time writing in Devon. His short stories soon brought the financial security of a New Yorker contract.

Trevor's early novels had a London setting. They are richly comical, yet display an underlying pessimism. There is a Dickensian quality to his gallery of misfits and eccentrics: Basil Jaraby in *The Old Boys*, who keeps budgerigars and turns out to be a child molester; the con-man Studdy conspiring with Nurse Clock in *The Boarding-House* (1965); the adulterous Eva Bolsover and Septimus Tuam in *The Love Department* (1966).

Trevor's ability to see events from a woman's viewpoint was underlined in his next three novels. In *Mrs Eckdorf in O'Neill's Hotel* (1969), a self-destructive photo-journalist seeks the cause of a Dublin hotel's decline. London is again the setting for *Miss Gomez and the Brethren* (1971), about a religious fanatic from Jamaica, and *Elizabeth Alone* (1973), in which four unhappy women meet in a hospital ward.

Much of Trevor's reputation comes from his short stories. His first collection, *The Day We Got Drunk on Cake*, was published in 1967. *The Ballroom of Romance* followed in 1972. Its title story, later filmed, is a moving recollection of a rural Ireland in which a middle-aged spinster finds her illusions of love destroyed as she tends her crippled father. Later collections include *Angels at the Ritz* (1975), *Beyond the Pale* (1981), and *The News from Ireland* (1986).

In *The Children from Dynmouth* (1976), which won the Whitbread Award, Trevor's portrayal of the 15-year-old blackmailer Timothy Gedge evoked comparisons with Pinkie in Graham Greene's *Brighton Rock*. In *Other People's Worlds* (1980) a widow is deceived into marrying a minor actor who deserts her. The overall impression is of alienation and despair.

Trevor is sometimes described as an Anglo-Irish writer, but his parents came from modest farming stock and not from the "big house" to which he turned in *Fools of Fortune* (1983), another Whitbread winner. It is possibly his finest novel, a story of doomed love set against the broader canvas of Ireland's troubled history. Trevor dealt less successfully with recent violence in his play *Scenes from an Album* (1981).

Ireland's history also looms large in *The Silence in the Garden* (1988), recounting the decline of a once prosperous Protestant family. In a typical mosaic of impressions and memories the secrets of the past emerge. *Felicia's Journey* (1994) brought Trevor another Whitbread award.

Trevor's writing has taken many forms. *Nights at the Alexandra* (1987) is an elegiac novella, in which an ageing bachelor looks back on his youthful infatuation with the wife of a German who, in World War II, builds a cinema in a small Irish town. In 1991 Trevor combined two novellas, *Reading Turgenev* and *My House in Umbria*, under the title *Two Lives*.

He has also written a number of plays for radio and television, and has adapted for television the work of authors such as Charles Dickens, Thomas Hardy, Graham Greene and Elizabeth Bowen (*see page 82*), with all of whom his own work shows some affinity. In *A Writer's Ireland: Landscape in Literature* (1984) he examined other writers' response to the Irish landscape. *Excursions in the Real World* (1993) brings together many of the entertaining autobiographical reminiscences which he has contributed to magazines. In 1999, Trevor became the fourth recipient of the David Cohen British Literature Prize, awarded for a lifetime's achievement and previously given to V. S. Naipaul, Harold Pinter and Muriel Spark.

BRIAN FRIEL

1929–

Friel was born in Killyclogher, near Omagh, Co. Tyrone, on 9 January 1929. His father was a schoolteacher, and in 1939 the family moved to Derry, where Friel was educated at St. Columb's College. He went to St. Patrick's College, Maynooth, but chose not to enter the priesthood, and in 1950 became a teacher in Derry. Ten years later, he opted for full-time writing, and settled in Co. Donegal.

His short stories had begun to appear in the *New Yorker*, and collections were published as *The Saucer of Larks* (1962) and *The Gold in the Sea* (1966). On the stage, his first critical success was the Abbey Theatre's production of *The Enemy Within* (1962), set in St. Columba's sixth century monastery on the Scottish island of Iona. In 1963, Friel spent six months at the new Tyrone Guthrie Theatre in Minneapolis.

Philadelphia, Here I Come!, staged by the Gaiety Theatre in Dublin in 1964, first demonstrated the innovative stagecraft which would mark all his plays, and brought him international success. It is set in Ballybeg, an imagined Donegal village which appears in other plays. It deals with emigration and exile, and with the inadequate communication of father and son. As young Gar O'Donnell prepares to leave for America, he reflects on the loneliness of his life. Gar is played by two actors, and Public Gar and Private Gar (the latter invisible to the rest of the cast but not to the audience) debate their shared life throughout the play. Philadelphia, they fear, will be no better than Ballybeg.

Loneliness and lack of communication also inform Friel's next two plays, *The Loves of Cass McGuire* (1966) and *Lovers* (1967). Cass Maguire is returning to the Ireland she left many years ago. A blowzy New York waitress, she is unacceptable to her brother, who puts her into an old people's home, where she relives unhappy memories. *Lovers* comprises two pessimistic short plays, *Winners* and *Losers*.

Friel continued to write interesting plays with varying success. In *Crystal and Fox* (1968) a travelling theatre provides the setting for marital breakdown. *The Mundy Scheme* (1969) satirically suggests solving Ireland's economic problems by turning the depopulated West into an enormous international cemetery. In *The Gentle Island* (1971) an isolated community have voted to quit their island home.

Friel had spent much of his life in the city which he, as a Roman Catholic, would always think of as Derry rather than Londonderry. In 1972, when a civil rights march ended with British soldiers killing thirteen civilians in what became known as Bloody Sunday, Friel responded with *The Freedom of the City* (1973). When a similar march in 1970 is dispersed, three demonstrators take refuge in the city's Guildhall, only to be shot as terrorists when they emerge. *Volunteers* (1975) also had a topical origin, the controversy over a proposed office block at Wood Quay, an archaeologically important site of Viking settlement in Dublin.

Friel returned to Ballybeg with *Living Quarters* (1977) and *Aristocrats* (1979), each involving a painful family reunion. In *Faith Healer* (1979), one of his most powerful and innovative plays, Frank Hardy meets his death in Ballybeg when he fails to cure. Unusually the play consists of four monologues. Frank's manager begins and ends the play; Frank and his wife, both speaking from the grave, also make solo appearances. Each character sees the past in a different way.

Translations (1980), an international success, depicts a hedge school in Ballybeg in 1833. The arrival of Royal Engineers of the Ordnance Survey, anglicising Irish names as they map, sets up a conflict between two cultures. The play employs a clever theatrical device in that, while Irish and English struggle to comprehend each other's language, all the actors are actually speaking English. The play was first staged in Derry by Field Day, a theatrical company founded by Friel and the actor Stephen Rea, which has since become an important cultural influence in Ireland.

Friel's later work has included a number of adaptations, notably from the Russian authors Chekhov and Turgenev. He returned to the clash between Irish and English cultures in *Making History* (1988), a dramatisation of the life of Hugh O'Neill, who led the "Flight of the Earls" to exile in 1607.

His most successful recent play is *Dancing at Lughnasa* (1990), yet another memory play set in Ballybeg. Subsequently filmed, it recalls through the eyes of an illegitimate son the hard lives of five unmarried sisters who briefly succumb to the spell of the pagan harvest festival of Lughnasa.

Later plays include *Wonderful Tennessee* (1993), *Molly Sweeney* (1994) and *Give Me Your Answer, Do!* (1997).

EDNA O'BRIEN

| 1930–

Edna O'Brien was born in Tuamgraney, Co. Clare, on 15 December 1930. She was educated locally and at the Convent of Mercy in Loughrea, Co. Galway, before moving to Dublin, where she qualified in pharmacy. Soon afterwards she met and married the American novelist Ernest Gébler, settling in London, but the marriage was dissolved in 1967.

O'Brien had always intended to become a writer, and her first novel, *The Country Girls*, was an immediate success when it was published in 1960. The two girls, Kate and Baba, get themselves expelled from their strict convent school and escape to sinful Dublin. Kate's romance with the solicitor known as Mr Gentleman comes to nothing, but in *The Lonely Girl* (1962) she is finally seduced by a film director before leaving for England with Baba. The novel was filmed as *Girl with Green Eyes* and republished under that title. *Girls in Their Married Bliss* followed in 1963.

The three novels offer a compelling picture, as comical as it is sad, of the Irish puritanism from which the country girls try to escape. Not surprisingly, they were banned under the Irish Republic's stringent censorship laws. When they were published as a trilogy in 1986 O'Brien added an bleak epilogue describing Kate's suicide and Baba's empty life.

Inevitably, O'Brien's later novels lack the youthful freshness that made her early work so appealing. They show the same gift for dialogue and characterisation, but are altogether more sombre. The heroine of *August Is a Wicked Month* (1964) is separated from her husband, who dies with their son in an accident while she contracts venereal disease during an affair in France. Violent deaths feature in such books as *Casualties of Peace* (1966) and *The High Road* (1988). *House of Splendid Isolation* (1994) is untypically topical in dealing with an IRA terrorist and the woman whose house he invades.

O'Brien has published several collections of short stories, including *Mrs. Reinhardt* (1978), *A Fanatic Heart* (1984) and *Lantern Slides* (1990). She has written extensively for cinema and television, sometimes adapting her own work. A valuable collaboration has been with the British director Desmond Davis on films of *Girl with Green Eyes* (1963), *The Country Girls* (1983), and *I Was Happy Here* (1965), whose heroine is yet another victim of an unsympathetic male. A travel book, *Mother Ireland* (1976), is a sharply observed commentary on her homeland.

SEAMUS HEANEY

1939–

Heaney was born in Co. Derry on 13 April 1939. His father was a farmer and cattle-dealer, and Heaney was the eldest of nine children. He attended the nearby Anahorish School until he was twelve, when he went as a boarder to St. Columb's College in Derry. He then studied English Language and Literature at Queen's University in Belfast, graduating with first class honours in 1961.

Like many young Roman Catholics who later made a mark in the world, Heaney was a beneficiary of Northern Ireland's post-war Education Act. In 1962 he joined the staff of St. Thomas's Intermediate School in Ballymurphy, one of Belfast's most deprived Catholic districts. Its headmaster was Michael McLaverty, a respected author of novels and short stories, who introduced Heaney to the work of Patrick Kavanagh (*see page 89*). Heaney realised that he too could find poetic inspiration in a not dissimilar rural background.

He was also encouraged by the poet Philip Hobsbaum, who had recently joined the English department at Queen's University. Hobsbaum brought together a group of young poets (among them Michael Longley and Derek Mahon) who met to discuss each other's work. Heaney's poems began to appear in newspapers and magazines, and in 1966 Faber & Faber published *Death of a Naturalist*, which won the Somerset Maugham Award and other literary prizes. When Hobsbaum moved to Glasgow in 1966, Heaney was appointed to a lectureship in his place. A second volume of verse, *Door into the Dark*, followed in 1969, by which time Northern Ireland had entered on the seemingly unending violence of "the Troubles".

Heaney had mixed freely with Protestants in his rural childhood, but he had always been conscious that Catholics were an underprivileged minority. He supported the civil rights movement, and even wrote a satirical song "Craig's Dragoons" following a clash between police and demonstrators. A later song, "The Road to Derry", lamented the dead of Bloody Sunday in 1972, but his verse has seldom been so political. However, if Heaney's early volumes concentrated on sensuous descriptions of farm life – ploughing, digging potatoes, churning butter and the like – his prose writing and broadcasting were outlets for a Catholic's sense of anger.

Heaney spent 1970–71 at the University of California at Berkeley. After a further year in Belfast, he gave up his lectureship and moved with his family to the greater safety of a cottage near Ashford, Co. Wicklow. His work continued to enjoy critical acclaim. *Wintering Out* (1972) was followed by *North* (1975), which won the Duff Cooper Prize. The collection of *Bog Poems* (1975) acknowledged a debt to P. V. Glob's *The Bog People*, a study of Iron Age ritual killings in Jutland in which Heaney saw parallels with contemporary Ireland.

In 1975 Heaney returned to the security of a salaried post, lecturing at Carysfort Training College in Dublin. He remained there until 1981, and made his home in the city. A new collection, *Field Work*, appeared in 1979. It contained an elegy for the late American poet, Robert Lowell, from whom Heaney had received the Duff Cooper award. Lowell had held a poetry workshop at Harvard University, and Heaney was offered the opportunity to teach there for part of the year. In 1984 he was elected to the Boylston Chair of Rhetoric and Oratory, letting him divide his time between Ireland and America.

He remains a prolific writer. Later volumes of verse include *Station Island* (1984), *The Haw Lantern* (1987), *Seeing Things* (1991), and *The Spirit Level* (1996). There have been collections of *Selected Poems* (1980 and 1990) and *Preoccupations: Selected Prose* (1980). His translations have ranger from *Sweeney Astray* (1983), drawn from a medieval Irish poem, to *The Cure at Troy* (1990), from Sophocles' play *Philoctetes*. He co-edited two verse anthologies with Ted Hughes, the British Poet Laureate. In 1989, Heaney was elected to a five-year term as Professor of Poetry at Oxford University. A coveted distinction, it proved a precursor to the award of the Nobel Prize for Literature in 1995.

Lowell described Heaney as "the best Irish poet since W. B. Yeats" (*see page 52*), though he has contributed fewer memorable lines to everyday conversation. A part of his popularity is a modest but persuasive manner, as effective in a poetry reading as in a television documentary. Of his Irishness there is no doubt. When he was included in an anthology of contemporary British poetry, he replied with *An Open Letter* (1983), a poem pointing out that "My passport's green./No glass of ours was ever raised/To toast The Queen".

MAEVE BINCHY

1940–

Maeve Binchy was born in Dublin on 28 May 1940. She was educated at Holy Child Convent in Killiney, Co. Dublin, before taking an arts degree at University College, Dublin. She taught for a number of years at Pembroke School in Dublin, before moving into journalism in 1968. She began a long-running column in *The Irish Times*, and was adept at colourful descriptive reporting. Her journalism, with its shrewd recollection of conversation and comic detail, was immensely popular and foreshadowed the warm-hearted quality of her fiction.

She moved to London, and her first two collections of short stories were linked by the London Underground, *Central Line* (1977) and *Victoria Line* (1980). A similar pattern followed with her first Irish stories, *Dublin 4* (1982) and *The Lilac Bus* (1984). The latter deals with a group of passengers who return home from Dublin each weekend, and Binchy later adapted it for television. Here and elsewhere, she shows a command of the nuances of small town life in the Irish provinces.

Meanwhile she had taken her first step to become Ireland's most successful popular novelist. *Light a Penny Candle* (1982) was the first of a series of substantial and very readable novels which have won acclaim throughout the world. It was followed by *Echoes* (1985), *Firefly Summer* (1987), *Circle of Friends* (1991), later adapted for the cinema, *The Copper Beech* (1992), *The Glass Lake* (1994), *Evening Class* (1996) and *Tara Road* (1998). She married the English writer Gordon Snell in 1977, and has largely divided her life between England and Ireland.

Binchy is to a degree a romantic novelist, and her titles have a nostalgic ring. She deals with courtship and marriage, and is much concerned with the warm friendships which her vulnerable women have often forged in childhood. Her novels look back to a simpler Ireland of the 1950s and 1960s. But there is a darker side to her writing, for it was also an Ireland in which the lives of young women were much constrained by social and religious puritanism, and in which they could be victims of uncaring, alcoholic or violent men. Many of her heroines guard terrible secrets.

Binchy has also published several collections of her continuing *Irish Times* journalism, and her plays *End of Term* (1976) and *Half Promised Land* (1979) have been staged in Dublin. Her television work includes the prize-winning *Deeply Regretted By* (1976).

RODDY DOYLE

1958–

Doyle was born in Dublin on 8 May 1958. He was educated at St. Fintan's Christian Brothers School in Sutton, Co. Dublin, and at University College, Dublin. He then became a teacher at Greendale Community School in Kilbarrack, on the north side of Dublin, where he remained until 1993. Kilbarrack, the semi-rural village in which he had grown up, had succumbed to the spread of the city's housing estates. It would become the Barrytown of his novels.

With a friend who would later become his agent, he published *The Commitments* in Dublin in 1987 under the King Farouk (rhyming slang for book) imprint. It had a mixed reception from Irish reviewers, but within a year it was taken up by a London publisher. In chronicling the rise and fall of Jimmy Rabbitte's Irish soul band, the novel depends heavily on the foul-mouthed conversation of its working class Dubliners. Doyle's novels, showing an acute ear for the language of deprived housing estates, adapt well for cinema or television, as Alan Parker's film of *The Commitments* (1991) quickly demonstrated. Later volumes in the trilogy were also filmed.

The Snapper (1990) continues the story of the Rabbitte family, who were at the heart of *The Commitments*, and deals with the problems of the young unmarried Sharon becoming pregnant in an Ireland which has not wholly shed its Catholic puritanism. *The Van* (1991), in which the senior member of the Rabbitte family becomes an unaccustomed entrepreneur selling take-away food, continues the blend of dark comedy and social realism which makes Doyle's novels so effective. Its hero, Jimmy Rabbitte Senior, is one of the most memorable figures in modern Irish fiction.

The Van was shortlisted for the prestigious Booker Prize, which Doyle eventually won in 1993 with *Paddy Clarke Ha Ha Ha*. The novel, set in 1968 when Barrytown was still being built, deals with the breakdown of a marriage as it affects the ten-year-old child of the title. It is darker than the earlier books, as is *The Woman Who Walked into Doors* (1996), a version of a four-part television series, *Family* (1994), which centred on a hard-drinking Dubliner inflicting violence on his family.

In addition to adapting his own work for the screen, Doyle has written for the theatre. His plays *Brownbread* (1987) and *War* (1989) were successes for the Dublin-based theatre company Passion Machine.

INDEX OF NAMES

| MAIN ENTRIES IN BOLD